PUB STROLLS IN
WEST YORKSHIRE

Len Markham

COUNTRYSIDE BOOKS
NEWBURY BERKSHIRE

COUNTRYSIDE BOOKS
3 Catherine Road
Newbury, Berkshire

To view our complete range of books,
please visit us at
www.countrysidebooks.co.uk

ISBN 1 85306 669 9

Designed by Graham Whiteman
Maps by the author and redrawn by Techniset Typesetters
Photographs by the author unless otherwise stated

Typeset by Techniset Typesetters, Newton-le-Willows
Produced through MRM Associates Ltd., Reading
Printed in Italy

Contents

INTRODUCTION   6

WALK

1 WETHERBY – The Red Lion ($3^3/_4$ miles)   7

2 ILKLEY – The Crescent Hotel (4 miles)   10

3 CLIFFORD – The Old Star ($2^1/_2$ miles)   13

4 HAREWOOD – The Harewood Arms (7 miles)   16

5 RIDDLESDEN – The Bridge ($3^1/_4$ miles)   19

6 THORNER – The Beehive ($5^1/_2$ miles)   22

7 ELDWICK – Dick Hudson's (4 miles)   25

8 ABERFORD – The Arabian Horse ($4^3/_4$ miles)   28

9 BARWICK-IN-ELMET – The New Inn ($2^3/_4$ miles)   31

10 ADEL – The Lawnswood Arms ($4^1/_2$ miles)   34

11 ROUNDHAY PARK, LEEDS – The Mansion ($2^1/_2$ miles)   37

12 STANBURY – The Old Silent (2 miles)   40

13 CALVERLEY – The Elmwood ($4^1/_2$ miles)   43

14 HARECROFT – The Station ($2^1/_2$ miles)   46

15 LEEDS – Whitelocks (2 miles)   49

16 LEDSHAM – The Chequers ($4^1/_2$ miles)   52

17 TONG – The Greyhound ($4^1/_2$ miles)   55

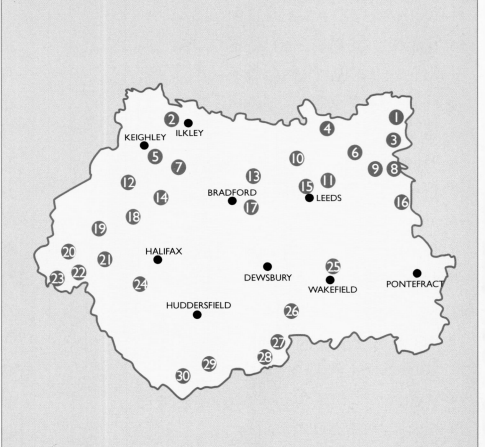

WALK

18 WAINSTALLS – The Withens Hotel (4$^1/_2$ miles)   58

19 CHISERLEY – The Hare and Hounds (2 miles)   61

20 TODMORDEN – The Staff of Life (2$^1/_2$ miles)   64

21 MYTHOLMROYD – The Shoulder of Mutton (3$^1/_2$ miles)   67

22 LUMBUTTS – The Top Brink (3 miles)   70

23 WALSDEN – The Waggon and Horses (2 miles)   73

24 GREETLAND – The Sportsman's Inn (2 miles)   76

25 WAKEFIELD – Henry Boon's (1$^1/_2$ miles)   79

26 MIDGLEY – The Black Bull (4$^1/_2$ miles)   82

27 CLAYTON WEST – The Junction (4$^3/_4$ miles)   85

28 DENBY DALE – The White Hart (2$^1/_2$ miles)   88

29 HOLMFIRTH – The Postcard (3 miles)   91

30 HOLME – The Fleece (2$^3/_4$ miles)   94

PUBLISHER'S NOTE

We hope that you obtain considerable enjoyment from this book; great care has been taken in its preparation. However, changes of landlord and actual closures are sadly not uncommon. Likewise, although at the time of publication all routes followed public rights of way or permitted paths, diversion orders can be made and permissions withdrawn.

We cannot, of course, be held responsible for such diversion orders and any inaccuracies in the text which result from these or any other changes to the routes nor any damage which might result from walkers trespassing on private property. We are anxious though that all details covering the walks and the pubs are kept up to date and would therefore welcome information from readers which would be relevant to future editions.

The sketch maps accompanying each walk are not always to scale and are intended to guide you to the starting point and give a simple but accurate idea of the route to be taken. For those who like the benefit of detailed maps, we recommend that you arm yourself with the relevant Ordnance Survey map in the Landranger series.

The mud on my boots was hardly dry following the publication *Pub Strolls in the Yorkshire Dales* when, hard on its heels, I got the call to lace up and head out once more. I couldn't have been more delighted! Born and brought up in the old West Riding, I know what is now West Yorkshire intimately having explored its surprisingly rural acres for over fifty years.

West Yorkshire is a diverse and rugged county, the sweat and sinew of its industrial past being matched by stunning scenery. For centuries, deep, well-watered valleys nurtured the textile industry, solid, unpretentious, stone-built towns and villages taking root under high fells that sweep up to the very backbone of England. In this comprehensive exploration of the now expanded county, I will take you on an intimate personal journey through peripheral villages, the old industrial heartland and over the ancient pack-horse routes, field paths and byways of the surrounding countryside. This collection of walks gives you all the beauty and grandeur of the Yorkshire Dales but with a steely edge. I have also included a magnificent route around the Harewood Estate — at 7 miles it's more than just a stroll, I admit, but well worth every step.

As only the footloose can, we will wander through two thoroughly modernised towns as well, visiting the fashionable precincts of Leeds and the leafy parts of Wakefield, seeing something of their histories and cultures, spurred on by a Yorkshire enthusiasm that, according to Bradford born J. B. Priestley, 'bred a race of mighty pedestrians'. Now I know why my first pair of bootees were made of leather!

On the way we will meet the ghost of the famous playwright and the spirits of a score of other celebrities as well. And we will visit some exciting, time-honoured pubs in out of the way places to enjoy the very best in real ales and wholesome food.

Using the route descriptions allied to the sketch maps, the walks are easily undertaken, all being on public rights of way. For convenience, they all start from a good pub or hotel whose telephone numbers are provided so that prospective customers can make advance enquiries about menus and opening times. Although parking details are also given, walkers should always seek permission from landlords before leaving their vehicles.

Finally, in this automotive, tele-cluttered, de-sensitised age, I invoke the ancestral call to legs in this stirring poem by an anonymous stroller of years gone by:

'Where hangs the deep blue vault of heaven
Star–powdered, flashing gold.
Where sing our hills the same sweet song,
The tale is never old.
Where flaming colours speed the sun,
Where westering shadows glow,
Where everything in nature calls,
Oh! Pack your kit and go.'

Len Markham

Wetherby

POOH STICKS AND A BRANCH LINE

The Red Lion

DIRECTIONS TO START: WETHERBY IS 13 MILES NORTH-EAST OF LEEDS AND IS EASILY REACHED ALONG THE A58 OR FROM THE A1. **PARKING:** PARK IN THE LARGE FREE 'WILDERNESS' CAR PARK ADJACENT TO THE RIVER.

Wetherby was an old coaching halt on the long diverted Great North Road (A1). Its impressive gateway is a monumental six-arched bridge, a listed structure first mentioned in 1233. A market town with an obvious pride in its heritage, Wetherby has preserved its weir, a salmon ladder and remnants of an old mill, a number of its picturesque former coaching inns, period shops and cottages bursting with floral colour during the summer months.

This walk of great contrasts begins at the bridge, our route soon leaving the bustle behind, a waterside path taking us along the banks and over the river on a pedestrian footbridge to a newly established bridlepath on the line of an abandoned railway. Through a leafy tunnel we are whisked into the countryside for a refreshment stop in the pretty village of Kirk Deighton – with a surprise view – before returning through fields and along another spur of the old railway back to Wetherby.

The Red Lion

Impressively situated, this stone-built, thoroughly modernised inn is very popular not least for its terrace with its grandstand views of the bridge and the River Wharfe. Stained glass, polished wood and pew-type seating give the interior an intimate feel, old photographs adding a touch of nostalgia. The inn offers a well-practised menu, the standard listings including steak and ale pie, chicken korma, gourmet lasagne, wild mushroom pasta, sausage and mash, chilli nachos, burgers and pizzas. The complementary ales are Tetley, Marston's Pedigree and rotating guest beers. Opening times Monday to Saturday are 11 am to 11 pm. Sunday hours are 12 noon to 10.30 pm. Telephone: 01937 582136.

The Walk

① Turn right from the inn, crossing the busy junction and the bridge (in 1233, Walter De Gray, Archbishop of York, forgave the sins of all those who contributed to the building of this structure) and go next right, following the signpost to the swimming pool. Within a few strides you will come to the steps down to the salmon ladder. Pass the pool and swing right and go through a metal kissing gate to the river bank. Swing left, following the water's edge to the footbridge.

② Go right over the footbridge to King George's Field and fork right on the concrete footway, leaving the park and climbing up steps to Linton Road. Go left on the footway for 50 yards and turn right

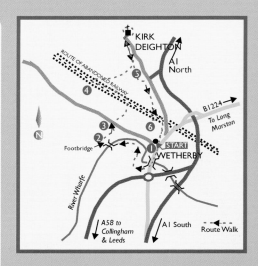

opposite the Station Gardens sign, to the car park.

③ Turn right over the parking area to the Harland Footpath and Cycleway sign. Using the former track of a line that once linked east Leeds and Harrogate, phase 1 of this Sustrans scheme connects Wetherby and Spofforth. Continue on the footpath and go under the bridge, following the left hand fork signposted to Spofforth. Go forward along the deep

PLACES OF INTEREST NEARBY

Wetherby Racecourse has an international reputation for its National Hunt meetings held every year between May and October. Telephone the Tourist Information Centre on 01937 582706 or 0113 247 7251 for details.

Just down the A1 from Wetherby is **Bramham Park**. It has its own world famous equestrian event in June when the Horse Trials are held. Its formal gardens, follies and nature trails can also be enjoyed. Open daily from February to September. Telephone: 01937 844265.

The six-arched bridge over the River Wharfe at Wetherby

Ashdale Lane and turn right for 150 yards.

⑤ Turn left, following a footpath sign over a stepped wall into a field. Veer left and right by the field corner and continue to the next corner, crossing a stile and going left at the edge of an estate to an access road. Turn right along Esk Gardens and keep going forward, crossing the next road to the right of Deighton Bar Post Office along a marked footpath. Swing to the right of a school and go left between a fence and back gardens. Pass a line of single garages and cross a further road, keeping straight ahead and following a public footpath sign. Swing left on a tarmac footway and go right, crossing a road and keeping straight forward uphill on Maple Drive. Go left on Oakwood Road and turn right. Keep going forward at the no vehicle entry sign over a bridge.

⑥ Drop down left to regain the Harland Way and turn right, following the 'Deighton Road ⅓ mile' sign. Walk on and follow a further Deighton Road sign left to the road. Cross and turn right using the footway. Continue into Wetherby, back to the inn.

cutting under the dense canopy of trees. At the next Harland Way sign, continue going forward to the third such sign.

④ Turn right and leave the Harland Way along an unsigned footpath, continuing hedgeside. Drop down to the field corner and swing right and left along the edge of the next field to a marker post. Go right along a broader track towards Kirk Deighton and merge with Ashdale Lane. Turn left into Kirk Deighton, passing the inviting Bay Horse pub. Continue along the lane climbing up to the Norman church of All Saints. Pass the church and go right, following a public footpath sign along the boundary wall. Looking north-east from here, can you make out the White Horse of Kilburn on a flank of the Hambleton Hills? Turn right and go through the churchyard, exiting through a gate back to the lane. Return to

Ilkley

A QUEST FOR THE SWASTIKA STONE

The Crescent Hotel

MAP REF: OS LANDRANGER 104 (GR 118478)	WALK 2	DISTANCE: 4 MILES

DIRECTIONS TO START: AT THE GATEWAY TO WHARFEDALE, ILKLEY IS NORTH-WEST OF BRADFORD ON THE A65 SKIPTON/LAKE DISTRICT TRUNK ROAD. **PARKING:** PARKING AT THE HOTEL IS FOR GUESTS ONLY. 'PAY AND DISPLAY' FACILITIES ARE AVAILABLE CLOSE BY (TURN LEFT IN FRONT OF THE HOTEL AND GO FIRST RIGHT).

Everyone can recite a verse from the internationally famous Yorkshire anthem 'Ilkley Moor Baht 'At'. Alfred J. Brown, the doyen of Yorkshire walkers, said it had 'the challenge of a charge and the pathos of a prayer', suggesting that the only place to sing it properly was on the moor itself with the legs 'moving rhythmically forward'. I cannot disagree with that! Dominating the town, the towering Ilkley Moor, or more properly Rombald's Moor, covers a vast upland south of the river. Ilkley was known in Roman times as Olicana but the occupation of this fascinating district pre-dates the Roman occupation by many centuries. Attesting to the activities of primitive Bronze Age peoples who worshipped their gods on the high moors are many cairns, stone circles and carvings on exposed rocks, the distinctive cup and ring symbol abounding. This journey into the past skirts the moor in a quest for the most intriguing symbol of all – the Swastika Stone.

The Crescent Hotel

A still fashionable former spa town once known as the Malvern of the North, Ilkley has a heritage of fine buildings. The Crescent Hotel, in a prominent roadside position opposite All Saints' church and the site of the Roman fort of Olicana, is one of the most attractive with its curving façade and entrance columns. Internally, it is elegant and stylish, providing restaurant facilities and a spacious bar and rear terrace area for more casual diners. Typically, the menu includes pan-fried duck breast, marinated lamb, Mediterranean vegetable platter, beef and ale pie, bacon chops and seared calves liver, the complementary ales being Theakston and Black Sheep. Bar opening times are from 11 am to 11 pm Monday to Saturday. Sunday hours are 12 noon to 10.30 pm. Telephone: 01943 600012.

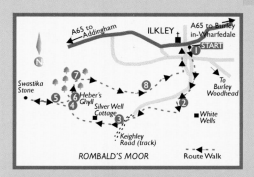

The Walk

① Go left from the hotel's front entrance along the busy street and swing left at the junction to the zebra crossing. Cross right and walk up Wells Road. Continue up the hill and go through the gate by the cattle grid, swinging right along the edge of the moor. On your right is the Millennium Maze whose design is based on the Swastika Stone. Pass the Yorkshire Water service reservoir and walk on for 250 yards.

② Go left at the White Wells Car Park sign on a rough track, climbing up. One hundred yards before the track arcs left over the bridge, go right on a path through the bracken and the bilberry and continue, merging with the track known as Keighley Road (no through road for vehicles). Cross Spicy Gill on the bridge and follow the track uphill left. Swing right and left.

③ Turn right on the public footpath marked 'Private Road' and go through a gate towards Silver Well Cottage, keeping left of the farm buildings and following the fence line and the forward footpath sign. Go through a gate and veer right through the bracken, swinging right towards the reservoir. Merge with a more substantial path and weave down to a planked bridge over the Black Beck.

④ Keep forward and go through a kissing gate and then walk on to the Swastika Stone. This is protected on three sides by a rusted fence and gate. Despite its

PLACES OF INTEREST NEARBY

Behind All Saints' church is the **Manor House**, a 16th century museum built on the site of the Roman fort – see the marker stones delineating the walls of the fort in the grounds. The museum displays both Roman and local history and has an exhibition detailing Ilkley's spa heritage. Open from Wednesday to Sunday in the afternoons. Telephone: 01943 600066.

The Millennium Maze, Ilkley

and after 100 yards swing right, following the public footpath sign downhill. Weave right and left and cross a series of bridges down to the bottom of the ghyll and the road.

⑦ Turn right and follow the public footpath sign uphill to 'Ilkley Moor'. Climb the steps and bear left, going through a fence gap, and swing right to a second fence gap, going through to a lane. Follow this down left for 500 yards and swing right into the woods, following the public footpath sign 'Panorama Woods'. Continue forward and leave the wood, passing Squirrels, and continue along the quiet Queen's Drive Lane.

incalculable age, the carvings on this stone are remarkably well preserved, although little is known about supposed magico-religious meaning of the symbols. Retrace your steps to the edge of the wood to where the route bifurcates.

⑤ Go left down to the rusted gate and turn right by the wall at the woodland edge, continuing to the Heber's Ghyll sign.

⑥ Turn left into the wood – green, mossy and cool – going through the kissing gate

⑧ Go left and arc right on the bend, swinging left down Parish Ghyll Walk. Drop down and cross the next road, swinging right along Parish Ghyll Drive and continuing along Albany Walk. At the end of this street, go left through a kissing gate and follow the landscaped path alongside the beck down into the town. Follow the outward route back to the hotel.

Clifford

THE EYE FULL TOWER

The Old Star

| MAP REF: OS LANDRANGER 105 (GR 429443) | WALK 3 | DISTANCE: 2½ MILES |

DIRECTIONS TO START: CLIFFORD IS EQUIDISTANT FROM BOSTON SPA AND BRAMHAM. ACCESS IS VIA EITHER VILLAGE SIGNPOSTED EASTWARDS OFF THE A1.
PARKING: PARK IN THE PUB CAR PARK OR ON-STREET.

An inconspicuous and retiring neighbour of fashionable Boston Spa, Clifford is a village of solid, unpretentious stone cottages and converted farmsteads, one dramatic building drawing the curious from far and wide. Saint Edward's church was erected between 1845 and 1848, its mighty tower being a later addition. An imposing Romanesque-style edifice, more fitted to an Italian piazza than rustic West Yorkshire, it soars above the surrounding lanes, its grandeur reflecting the status of some of its benefactors. A hive of religious activity, Clifford also has a Methodist chapel and another notable church, St Luke's, built between 1840 and 1842.

Passing the old Grimston's flax mill with its rusted waterwheel, this pleasant and leisurely route crosses the Green Beck, taking hedgeside paths and a farm track to Oglethorpe Whin Covert, returning through the wood to a quiet lane back to the village.

The Old Star

Almost in the shadow of Saint Edward's tower, the homely Old Star is built of local limestone like its soaring neighbour. Popular with walkers, it has cosy twin bars simply decorated with old photographs and a collection of water jugs. Its tried and tested menu is big on traditional staples such as beef steaks, home-made steak pie, gammon steak, roast chicken and scampi. The house ales are all from the Sam Smith brewery. Opening times Monday to Saturday are 11.30 am to 3 pm and 7 pm to 11 pm daily. Sunday opening is 12 noon to 3 pm and 7 pm to 10.30 pm. Telephone: 01937 842486.

③ Turn right on the track, walking on towards Oglethorpe Whin Covert. Pass the wood corner and proceed for 150 yards.

The Walk

① Turn right down High Street, passing St Edward's church, and swing hard right on Old Mill Lane, going left past the three tall fir trees to cross the Green Beck. The derelict machinery on the left of the road once powered the flax mill which in recent years has been converted to residential accommodation. Swing right, passing Mill Pond Cottage, for 50 yards.

② Turn left, following a public footpath sign on a broad track, swinging right between a fence and a hedge. Continue at the side of a second field and walk under the power lines. At the end of the field swing left on a track for 100 yards and turn right, following a public footpath sign, on a hedgeside path to a broad track.

The tower of St Edward's church soars above surrounding lanes

PLACES OF INTEREST NEARBY

The burial ground of Clifford's **St Luke's church** is a designated haven for wildlife.

Nearby **Boston Spa** has a number of speciality shops, café bars and restaurants. This former spa town has good coarse fishing on the River Wharfe and some delightful riverside walks. The **Lower Wharfe Angling Centre** supplies day tickets, tackle and bait. Telephone: 01937 844260.

④ Turn right into the wood, following the footpath sign on a rough loggers' access track. After 300 yards, turn right and continue to the wood edge.

⑤ Exit the wood and steer left over a field, following the footpath sign and aiming equidistant between an oak tree and a pylon. Walk on to the lane, cross and follow the footpath sign, veering left onto the edge of the next field, continuing on a path to the lane.

⑥ Turn right on the lane, later following the outward route back to the pub.

Harewood

CARR, KITES AND CAPABILITY

The Harewood Arms

MAP REF: OS LANDRANGER 104 (GR 322452)	WALK 4	DISTANCE: 7 MILES

DIRECTIONS TO START: HAREWOOD IS ON THE A61 MIDWAY BETWEEN LEEDS AND HARROGATE.
PARKING: PARKING TO THE REAR OF THE HAREWOOD ARMS IS STRICTLY LIMITED TO CUSTOMERS ONLY AND AT BUSY PERIODS IS CONTROLLED BY A BARRIER (TOKENS AVAILABLE FROM THE BAR). ALTERNATIVELY, PARK HALFWAY ROUND THE ROUTE ON ECCUP MOOR ROAD OPPOSITE BANK HOUSE FARM – SEE MAP – STARTING THE WALK AT POINT 5.

Harewood village is dominated by the ancestral home of the Earl of Harewood, his vast estate extending to thousands of acres flanking Wharfedale, north of Leeds. The magnificent Harewood House was begun in 1759 to designs by John Carr, the equally inspired gardens and grounds coming under the spell of landscaping genius Capability Brown. A benign legacy of history enables walkers to ramble through the estate on a network of public paths, sweeping views of Wharfedale, the mansion and stately groves of trees all adding to a notably regal experience.

On a country lane, this walk takes us along the edge of the reservoir at Eccup and on between ancient hedgerows, colourful drifts of wild flowers in season and scores of self-sown oaks contrasting splendidly with the formal plantings of the estate.

The Harewood Arms

Stone-built and elegant with neat lawns and gardens that would impress old Capability himself, this superior inn sits alongside the A61 opposite Harewood's imperial gates. Restrained luxury typifies the attractive polished wood and chintz interiors whose walls are adorned with royal photographs. The inn offers modern and sophisticated restaurant and bar menus, typical inclusions being queen scallops, pork and bacon roll with provençale sauce, spicy lamb kebabs, Mediterranean vegetable filo tart and meatballs with herb dumplings. Two distinctive ales from the Sam Smith brewery are on tap – Old Brewery and Sovereign bitters. Opening times are 11 am to 11 pm daily. Telephone: 0113 288 6566.

The Walk

① Cross the road from the inn and turn right, going next left down Church Lane. Keep to the right of East Lodge and keep forward, following the bridleway sign for 200 yards to a gate. Go through and continue on the metalled lane, walking on to cross a cattle grid. There are glorious views of Wharfedale from here, the prospect including the River Wharfe, Almscliff Crag, Arthington Viaduct and Rombald's Moor. Keep going forward left, dropping down between high banks until you come to the signs.

② At the point where the route bifurcates, follow the sign left, walking up to the cattle grid. Cross and walk on over the field to the next cattle grid,

crossing and continuing straight forward to pass the Harewood Yard buildings converted from the former Home Farm to business use. See the 'inebriated' window sills! Drop down and continue through the gate, crossing a stream. Bear left, right and left uphill, turning right off the metalled lane at the Bothy entrance on a signposted track. Drop down, passing the old walled garden, go through a gate and swing left and right, walking uphill on a track at the edge of a wood towards a cottage. Go forward through the gate by the cottage and enter woodland right, climbing up to a path. Go right and after

PLACES OF INTEREST NEARBY

Harewood House is open from Easter to October. It offers stately home attractions including a unique collection of Chippendale furniture, bird garden, tropical rain forest exhibition, adventure playground, garden centre, gift shops, restaurant and picnic area. Telephone: 0113 288 6225.

Wharfedale seen from the Harewood Estate

400 yards go sharp left uphill, merging with a path from the right and continuing to public bridleway signs. Turn right here and drop down on a track, passing the farm buildings.

③ At the Harewood Estate sign, keep going forward, following the marked route on a track, climbing and passing a wood on the left at the edge of a long field. Pass through a gap in the fence, keep forward between hedges and go through a gate onto the access to Eccup Treatment Works (on your left).

④ Go right down the quiet Eccup Moor Road for about 1 mile.

⑤ Turn right 150 yards past Bank House Farm, following a public bridleway sign through a gate. After 200 yards, steer left off the concrete track, swinging left between hedges. The next marked path off left would take you to the New Inn at Eccup. Swing right and follow the track, swinging left and then right through a gate, going left in the field corner, following an arrow marker on a post. Go through the next gate and swing left, dropping down to a marker post. Go right, following the sign on a track, and go next left at the Harewood Estate sign (point 3), following the outward route back to the inn.

Riddlesden

UP HILL AND DOWN ALE

The Bridge

| MAP REF: OS LANDRANGER 104 (GR 074423) | WALK 5 | DISTANCE: 3¼ MILES |

DIRECTIONS TO START: RIDDLESDEN IS IN AIREDALE NEAR THE NORTH-EASTERN OUTSKIRTS OF KEIGHLEY OFF THE A650. THE PUB IS PROMINENTLY SITUATED ON THE B6265 OVERLOOKING THE RIVER AIRE. **PARKING:** PARK IN THE PUB CAR PARK.

The congested Aire valley accommodates the river, the Leeds and Liverpool Canal, a railway line and the busy A650 trunk road, a shortage of level ground seeing many of Riddlesden's homes built on terraced plots stretching to the fringes of Rombald's Moor. Originally a village of yeoman farmers, Riddlesden developed as a centre for cottage weaving, its prosperity booming with the coming of the canal in 1774 and the creation of textile mills. Weighing in at over one and a quarter tons, the famous Airedale Heifer lived in the town until 1830 when she was slaughtered after suffering a severe injury.

This short, but thoroughly absorbing walk begins by the river and takes in a short section of the canal before climbing up on field paths to the hilltop hamlet of West Morton. The inward route descends on a historic footpath. Now considerably overgrown, Bury Lane was one of the main pedestrian links in the area for centuries, its former status honoured by its own nameplate.

The Bridge

A large and accommodating roadside house named after the eponymous crossing of the river just a few yards from its door, this inn has been thoroughly modernised in recent years providing light and airy dining, its interior enhanced by an inviting conservatory. The varied menu includes a range of grilled steaks, steak and ale pie, steak and mushroom suet pudding, lamb shank, chicken tikka masala, cod mornay and a good selection of vegetarian options. The ale choices are Tetley and Calders. Opening hours are 11 am to 11 pm daily (12 noon to 10.30 pm on Sundays). Telephone: 01535 653144.

The Walk

① Turn left from the pub along the B6265, cross the bridge on the footway and pass the end of Grange Road. After 200 yards, go left on Bar Lane and turn right at the top, walking down the canal footpath to the lock.

② Turn left over the lock gates and climb uphill on Granby Lane. At the junction turn right down Carr Lane and at the junction with Southlands Avenue turn right for 40 yards, going next left along the top of Daleside Road. What confronts you here given a few special effects – the hoot of an owl here and the sound of moaning from the bushes – could be a set from a Hammer Horror film. The carved letters on the long abandoned entrance pillars read 'ISOLATION HOSPITAL'. Its extensive grounds are extensively overgrown and rather sinister. Go left by

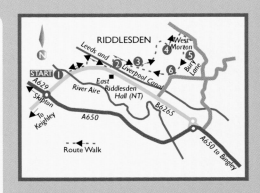

the gates, following a signed footpath for 200 yards.

③ Turn left through a wall gap into a field, following a wall-painted arrow marker, steering right and following a beck up. Go through a second wall gap by a gate and swing right on a bridge over the beck, passing Morton Pumping Station and keeping forward towards the farm buildings and the cottages in West Morton. Go through a gap by a gate, following a yellow arrow marker, and pass the cottages.

④ Turn next left uphill on a track and

PLACES OF INTEREST NEARBY

Almost on the route of this walk, at the bottom of Granby Lane, is **East Riddlesden Hall**, a National Trust property built as a merchant's house at the time of the Civil War. It has an outstanding collection of embroidery and vernacular oak furniture, a 17th century barn, a walled garden with a herb border and a tranquil pond. Open from April to October at weekends and on Tuesdays and Wednesdays (also Bank Holiday Mondays, Thursdays during July and August and Good Friday) in the afternoons. Telephone: 01535 607075.

The Leeds and Liverpool Canal.

swing hard right and left to the lane. Turn right on the lane for 220 yards and turn right again, following a public bridleway sign and passing Brownhill Bungalow. Drop down left, passing Bates Barn. Swing left by Dean Hole Farm for 150 yards and go left on a path between low walls.

⑤ Turn right on Bury Lane, continuing downhill through several gates to the junction.

⑥ Turn right along Carr Lane and, at the junction, continue forward over South View, going through a wall gap onto a path. Keep forward and continue, going through an old gate by the perimeter of the Isolation Hospital. Retrace your steps back to the pub from here.

Thorner

ALL ROADS LEAD TO POMPOCALI

The Beehive

MAP REF: OS LANDRANGER 104 (GR 376400)	WALK 6	DISTANCE: 5$\frac{1}{2}$ MILES

DIRECTIONS TO START: THORNER IS ABOUT 8 MILES NORTH-EAST OF LEEDS. TAKE THE LEEDS RING ROAD (A6120) AND THEN EITHER THE A64 OR THE A58 – THORNER IS SIGNPOSTED OFF BOTH TRUNK ROADS.
PARKING: PARK EITHER IN THE PUB CAR PARK TO THE REAR OR ON THE BROAD MAIN STREET.

In the old days, father would escape the grime of a Leeds oil-can factory for a pint at the Beehive, and I would cadge a ride in uncle's Morris Oxford to delight in a ginger beer and a romp in the beck. I am happy to announce that the ancient ford at the western end of Main Street is still there. But walkers beware lingering here. Outside commuter hours, this relaxing place has all the rush of a tipped sombrero.

Our fields and woodlands walk leads us beside the Scarcroft Beck to the remains of an intriguing hilltop settlement marked on the larger scale Pathfinder map SE24/34 as Pompocali. Much smaller, but every bit as mysterious as the prehistoric fort at Maiden Castle in Dorset, it overlooks the line of a Roman road whose course we follow into the Stubbing Moor Plantation. The last mile takes us along a bridle track to a crossing over the Thorner Beck and back to the village, passing the fascinating church.

The Beehive

This pub's name evokes languid days of hot sun and dawdle, and food at the Beehive is similarly inspired, the Spanish influenced menu listing daily specials such as paella, boqueronnes, anchovies, marinated mussels, patatas bravas and mejillones. In winter, try the ribeye steak, the steak and ale pie or the sausage, mash and onion gravy. Meals can be taken either in the stylish dining room which overlooks the water meadows to the front or in the adjacent bars. The bar top line up is John Smith's, Tetley and Black Sheep. Opening times are 11.30 am to 3 pm and 6.30 pm to 11 pm Monday to Friday. Weekend openings are 11 am to 11 pm on Saturday and 12 noon to 10.30 pm on Sunday. Telephone: 0113 289 2711.

The Walk

① Turn right from the inn on the footway and swing right on Main Street at the bend near the ford, continuing to the Fox public house. Go left, following a public footpath sign down a narrow ginnel, and continue through three kissing gates past the church conversion to the lane. Turn left for 100 yards.

② Turn right, following a public footpath sign to 'Scarcroft', walking uphill to a gate. Go through and left over a field downhill on a well-trodden footpath towards woodland. At the next field go down steps and keep left, following the yellow arrow marker, entering the wood via a kissing gate.

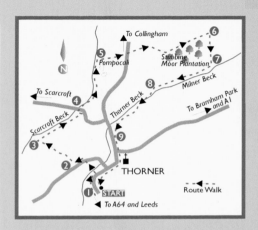

③ Turn right on the woodland track, swing left to a gate and go through, passing Oaklands Manor, continuing on the lane to the junction. Go left on the descending lane, swinging right and left and cross the Scarcroft Beck on a bridge, passing the tennis courts and climbing up for 200 yards to the 'Scarcroft and Nature Reserve' public footpath sign.

④ Turn right, following the track, and veer right at the entrance to Moat Hall to a gate. Go through, following a public footpath sign over a small field and heading for a yellow-tipped marker post. Go through a gate and turn left on a track, passing under a defunct railway bridge. Cross a stile and keep forward at the field edge, passing derelict mill buildings, and steer left downhill to a gate and a stile. Cross, arcing right by the beck. Keep on the high ground and walk on parallel with the beck to the ramparts of Pompocali. Drop down forward to a stile and cross.

⑤ Turn right on a track and continue to the lane and cross, continuing on the footpath fieldside (old Roman road) to a gate. Go through, walk on to a gate

Thorner village

opening, going through and continuing right towards Stubbing Moor Plantation. Enter the plantation on the broad path and continue to a junction with a track at the plantation edge.

⑥ Turn right, following a public bridleway sign, and swing right and left between field boundaries to a further bridleway sign.

⑦ Turn right on a track and walk on for just over ¹/₂ mile to a public footpath sign.

PLACES OF INTEREST NEARBY

Just down the lane from Thorner is **Bramham Park**, an estate known widely for its annual Horse Trials held in June. Its grounds – formal gardens, follies and nature trails – are open daily to the public from February to September. Telephone: 01937 844265.

⑧ Turn left, following the sign hedgeside downhill towards Milner Wood. Drop down steps and cross the Thorner Beck on a footbridge, swinging right, and follow the path left away from the beck to a stile. Cross right and, keeping roughly parallel with the trees to your right, follow the valley of the beck up, gradually arcing left. Merge with a rough track and follow the line of a broken hedge to a stile. Cross and follow a yellow arrow marker and a hedge and veer left at the next yellow arrow marked post to cut off the corner of the field, dropping down to a kissing gate. Go through and drop down to Milner Lane.

⑨ Turn left, using the footway, along the lane and swing right at the junction, passing St Peter's church. Continue down Thorner's Main Street, back to the inn.

Eldwick

MEDITATE WITH THE TWELVE APOSTLES

Dick Hudson's

| MAP REF: OS LANDRANGER 104 (GR 124421) | **WALK 7** | DISTANCE: 4 MILES |

DIRECTIONS TO START: ISOLATED FROM NEARBY ELDWICK VILLAGE, DICK HUDSON'S IS ON THE SOUTHERN EDGE OF ROMBALD'S MOOR BETWEEN ILKLEY AND BINGLEY. FROM THE EAST, TAKE THE A660 TO OTLEY, THE A6038 TO MENSTON AND THEN MINOR ROADS. FROM THE WEST TAKE THE A629 TO KEIGHLEY AND THEN MINOR ROADS FROM RIDDLESDEN. **PARKING:** PARK IN THE PUB CAR PARK.

Probably the best-known pub in the whole of West Yorkshire, Dick Hudson's stands at the foot of the famous Rombald's Moor. An outpost of Eldwick and the vast conurbation of Bingley, Baildon, Shipley and Bradford to the south, it has stood as a moorland portal for generations of textile factory workers, vast numbers making the weekend pilgrimage across the heather to Ilkley.

Reaching a height of over 1,300 ft, Rombald's Moor is a wilderness with many dark secrets, prehistoric remains abounding. This linear walk (2 miles each way) has the Bronze Age stone circle known as the Twelve Apostles as its destination. Set on a bank of earth and stones near the summit of the moor, this circle of irregularly spaced standing stones or orthostats, is 52 ft in diameter. I have also described the full route to Ilkley ($7\frac{1}{2}$ miles in total from the pub to the town and back) for walkers who want to complete the classical route of old.

Dick Hudson's

More formally known as the Fleece, this attractive, big-hearted pub, named after a landlord of 1850, has saved more lives than the Mountain Rescue, its reviving platters of ham and eggs going down in history. Once served from a 30 inch frying pan from 6 o'clock in the morning to 11 o'clock at night, the legendary rashers, according to one aficionado, 'scented the air with the aroma of home fed ham so that the wanderers over the moor twitched their noses like camels coming to water and lengthened their stride for the last quarter of a mile.' The modern menu embraces steak and mushroom pie, lamb shoulder with rosemary, seafood stir-fry, a range of grilled steaks, hot spicy chicken goujons and the celebrated farmhouse gammon. The ale tally is Bass and Tetley. Daily opening times are from 12 noon to 11 pm (10.30 pm on Sundays). Telephone 01274 562554.

The Walk

① Turn left from the rear of the pub and go left to the junction, turning left again along the lane for 100 yards. Turn right through a wall gap, following the 'Dales Way Link' footpath sign. Follow the path up to a gate and go through onto the moor. Eldwick Crag is to the left. Walk on the distinctive path left on the causeway through the heather up to the old boundary stone and proceed gradually right over Bingley Moor to merge with a wall.

② Cross through the wall gap and continue to the second old milestone, veering left on an ascending track up to the stone circle to the right of the path.

③ About face and retrace your steps on the outward route, back to the inn.

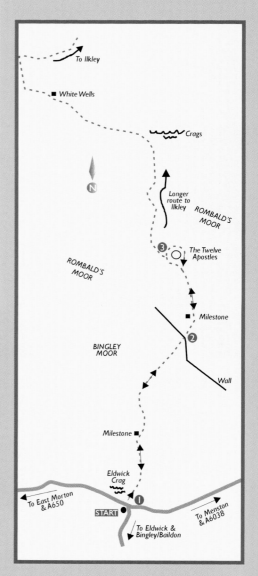

A milestone at the top of Bingley Moor

PLACES OF INTEREST NEARBY

Another internationally famous gourmet dish may be sampled in nearby Guiseley. Harry Ramsden established his fish and chip shop in the town in 1931 at White Cross and his original emporium still fries over 1 million portions annually of 'one of each' either in the restaurant or as take-away meals. Situated at the north of the town at the A6038/A65 junction, **Harry Ramsden's** is open every day. Telephone: 01943 879531.

In Bradford is the **Bradford Industrial Museum** displaying an original spinning mill, workers' housing and a working horse bus. Signposted from the Bradford ring road and the Harrogate road (A658). Open Tuesdays to Sundays and Bank Holiday Mondays. Telephone: 01274 631756.

The route into Ilkley from here follows a well-defined path left. Gradually drop down and merge with a path from the left. Keep forward, cross the Blackstone Beck at Gill Head and veer right, dropping down and steering to the left of the crags, continuing in the direction of the distinctive cluster of white-painted buildings – White Wells. Keep to the left of the buildings on the access track (refreshments at the weekend 'when the flag is flying'), swinging left to a bridge over a deeply clefted beck. Swing right on the track, passing the car parking area to the road. Turn right and go left, following the road into Ilkley centre. Retrace your steps to return to Eldwick.

Aberford

A RECONNOITRING RAMBLE

The Arabian Horse

MAP REF: OS LANDRANGER 105 (GR 433374)	WALK 8	DISTANCE: 4³/₄ MILES

DIRECTIONS TO START: ABERFORD IS NEAR THE A1(M) (LEAVE AT JUNCTION 48) BETWEEN FERRYBRIDGE AND WETHERBY. THE ARABIAN HORSE IS JUST NORTH OF THE COCK BECK BRIDGE. **PARKING:** PARK IN THE INN'S REAR CAR PARK OR ON-STREET.

(Photo courtesy of R. Hartley)

In the days when carriages and six thundered over the Great North Road, Aberford was a prime staging post, many weary travellers 'putting up' at the famous Arabian Horse with 'its quaint settles and picturesque interior'. Located at a strategic crossing of the Cock Beck, the village was protected by a formidable line of entrenchments, becoming an important halt on the Roman army's Ermine Street. Today, with direct access from the A1(M) blocked off, leafy Aberford is a place to dawdle.

Surprisingly rural and well-wooded, this undulating walk follows the lines of the ancient fortifications, leading on, through a former deer park, to Becca Hall and Potterton Hall. The return route over tracks and field paths breaches the old defence works, crossing the beck at the site of a former mill.

The Arabian Horse

A rare breed of inn, the only such named establishment in the whole of the UK, the 18th century Arabian Horse overlooks the village green, customers spilling out to enjoy its shaded bowers in the summer months. Originally called the Bay Horse, the inn was renamed after a string of Arabian stallions were stranded in the village on their way to the gallops in Masham in 1850. Stone-built with a massive open fireplace rediscovered during restoration work in 1975, it has large front and rear lounges serving mainly snack-type meals, typically variously filled baguettes, jacket potatoes, ham and eggs and fish and chips. The medley of ales includes Theakston, John Smith's and a weekly guest ale. Opening times are 11 am to 11 pm daily (12 noon to 10.30 pm on Sundays). Telephone: 0113 281 3312.

The Walk

① Cross the road, forking right to Becca Lane, continuing on the tarmacked lane past the gatehouse. Walk on to the second gatehouse, going forward between the ornamental entrance gate piers on a gravelled track into parkland. At the arrow marker on a post, go left at the edge of Becca Low Wood and swing right on a path to a gate. The imposing property to the right is Becca Hall. Prominent owners have included the Grammarys, the Carvill family and Sir Clement Markham KCB. Go through and swing right on a track to Becca Home Farm, continuing past the farm on a path, bearing left hedgeside for about 250 yards.

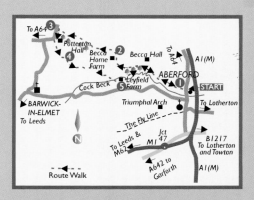

② Turn left on a field path towards a yellow-marker post, weave left and right bisecting two fields and head for a solitary tree. Steer right at the edge of the replanted portion of South Plantation, swinging right in the field corner and going left over a stile, following the yellow arrow marker. Go left at the yellow-tipped marker post and swing right by the hedge.

PLACES OF INTEREST NEARBY

The Fly Line – once a mineral railway linking coal mines in Garforth with Aberford – is now an inviting country path, wooded for most of its length. (Walk south uphill past the church and turn right opposite the Lotherton Road junction.) The Gascoigne family once lived in the long demolished Parlington Hall. Its site can be seen from the entrance to the fascinating Dark Arch, about ¾ mile west of Aberford down the Fly Line. See also the Light Arch. In 1783, the Gascoignes raised a triumphal arch to commemorate 'Liberty in N America Triumphant'. At the head of a long avenue of trees in Parlington Park it can be inspected by walking down the quiet drive opposite the old gatehouse about 250 yards west of Aberford down Barwick Road. The tympanum of this old house features a stone carved pike's head – part of the Gascoigne family crest.

The Gascoigne almshouses, Aberford

Go through the hedge gap and walk at the edge of Old Plantation. Potterton Hall can be glimpsed through the trees. Cross a stile to the right of the gateway in the corner of the field and veer right across the next field to the lane – stopped to through traffic.

③ Cross the stile left and continue on the lane, passing the entrance to Potterton Hall. Proceed through a gate, following the bridleway sign, on a broad track. Swing left on the track. The ancient entrenchments known as The Ridge and the hilltop village of Barwick-in-Elmet can be clearly seen from this point.

④ Go sharp right on a continuing farm track, swinging left for about 150 yards. Swing right through a copse on a track, dropping down, and go left for about 200 yards. Turn right and walk on to cross the Cock Beck on a bridge, going through a gate to a meadow. Steer left uphill, following the yellow direction arrows on a tree and a telegraph pole to a gate in the corner. Go through.

⑤ Go forward for 50 yards and go left opposite the farmyard, dropping down on a sunken track, going through a gate and swinging left to a bridge over the Cock Beck. A watermill was sited here. As well as dace and chub, the beck still yields the occasional trout. Cross, steering left across a meadow to a stile. Cross and take a field path right up towards Becca Low Wood, entering the wood on a track and swinging left to a gate. Go through and turn right on the outward route back to the inn.

Barwick-in-Elmet

IN THE STEPS OF KING EDWIN

The New Inn

MAP REF: OS LANDRANGER 104/105 (GR 400371)	WALK 9	DISTANCE: $2^3/_4$ MILES

DIRECTIONS TO START: BARWICK-IN-ELMET IS AROUND 8 MILES NORTH-EAST OF LEEDS. THE BEST ACCESS IS FROM THE A64 ROUNDABOUT AT SEACROFT. THE NEW INN IS AT THE SOUTH END OF MAIN STREET. **PARKING:** PARK ON-STREET.

Even the name of this former citadel village wraps round the consciousness like a bastion wall. The 2,000 year old Iron Age capital of a kingdom that before the Roman invasion held sway over vast tracts of northern England, Barwick-in-Elmet was protected by vast earthworks, dykes and entrenchments, the still distinctive Wendel Hill and the rearing motte in Hall Tower Field giving just a hint of the power of this stronghold of Celtic kings. Despite the encroachments of the nearby metropolis of Leeds, Barwick with its 14th century church and three popular pubs, retains its character and independent air, a centuries old maypole – the tallest in England – prize-winning summer floral displays and a network of rustic paths and lanes attracting many visitors from the city.

Using these ancient trackways, this walk skirts the old settlement of King Edwin, visiting the sites of the fortifications, their designation as 'Scheduled Ancient Monuments' preserving an unmolested haven for wildlife and rare flowers.

The New Inn

The smallest but the most intimate, friendly and chirpy of Barwick's trio of pubs, this cosy three-roomed house has been the favourite haunt of locals for decades. But beware. When this CAMRA award-winning little gem entertains the village football and cricket teams, it's full! One miniscule bar serves both the tap-room and the two interconnecting lounge bars whose rustic furniture includes tables cut from solid slabs of timber. John Smith's bitter is the favoured local brew but Chestnut Dark Mild and rotating guest beers are also on tap. The menu is simple and homespun, the choices ranging from speciality pies – meat and potato, chicken and ham and steak – to omelettes and roasts. Opening times on Monday to Saturday are 12 noon to 11 pm. Sunday opening is 12 noon to 3 pm and 7 pm to 10.30 pm. Telephone: 0113 281 2289.

The Walk

① Turn left from the inn down Chapel Lane, walking on the footway past the village hall and playing fields to the bend. Turn right, following the footpath sign on a track, continuing past the allotments to a kissing gate. Go through and veer left across a meadow. There are attractive views to the left of the village church. Go through a gate, cross a stream on a planked bridge and fork right over a second meadow to a stile, crossing to the road.

② Turn left on the road to the church and cross right to its entrance gate. All Saints has Norman elements and many

interesting connections with the Gascoigne family (see also Walk 8). The superb, stained glass memorial windows are particularly fascinating. Walk to the right of the porch and swing left, exiting the churchyard left and right through a gate onto Potterton Lane. Continue on the footway for about 400 yards.

③ Turn left, crossing the road, and walk down Meadow View, steering right of the access to Pear Tree Farm. Continue on a footpath, crossing two stiles, onto the

PLACES OF INTEREST NEARBY

Lotherton Hall and Bird Garden – a Leeds City Council property, this former home of the Gascoigne family (interesting connections in Barwick's All Saints' church) has period furniture, ceramics, textiles and art, together with walled gardens and a tropical bird sanctuary. At Lotherton, $3\frac{1}{2}$ miles south-east of Barwick-in-Elmet on the B1217. The hall and gardens are open from April to the end of December on Bank Holiday Mondays and Tuesday to Saturday 10 am to 5 pm (an hour earlier closing in winter); Sundays 12 noon to 4 pm. Telephone: 0113 281 3259. The Bird Garden is open all year, opening hours matching those of the hall.

A winter scene in Barwick-in-Elmet (courtesy of R. Hartley)

to find a footpath between the houses, continuing to a road, crossing and going slightly left down Carrfield Road to find a hidden footpath between numbers 52 and 54. Weave right and left on a leafy path to the main road.

⑥ Cross and proceed down Flats Lane. You can see Garforth church in the far distance. Just beyond the sloping agricultural land in front was the old Garforth Colliery. Turn left at the bottom of the lane down Gascoigne Avenue to the main road and turn right passing the end of Parlington Meadow, walking on a short distance to the bridge over the Long Lane Beck. Within living memory, otters thrived here.

⑦ Turn left at the edge of the housing estate, following the beck and a gravelled path to its end. Turn left uphill on Beck Meadow, going left at the summit. Continue for about 400 yards and go right on Richmonfield Garth, swinging right and left on a path to Chapel Lane. Turn left, back to the inn.

shoulder of Wendel Hill. This bulwark was protected at its base by a system of sluices that enabled the approaches to be flooded in times of danger. Undisturbed in hundreds of years, the hillside is a haven for rare orchids. Drop down right to a stile in the bottom and cross to the lane.

④ Turn left on the lane uphill and turn right on the quiet Rakehill Road, continuing for 400 yards to a footpath sign. Go left through a hedge gap, walking diagonally left up a sloping field to a gate. Turn right, following a hedge line uphill. Go left at the side of a house at the top to an estate road.

⑤ Turn right and swing left and right

Adel

GEM STONES

The Lawnswood Arms

<table>
<tr><td>MAP REF: OS LANDRANGER 104
(GR 270402)</td><td>WALK 10</td><td>DISTANCE: $4^1/_2$ MILES</td></tr>
</table>

DIRECTIONS TO START: ADEL IS NORTH OF THE LEEDS RING ROAD A6120 AND IS EASILY ACCESSED OFF THE A660. **PARKING:** PARK IN THE PUB CAR PARK.

Adel – the hill of Ada after the first Saxon colonist of this place – has been almost swamped as an anonymous suburb of Leeds but it steadfastly refuses to give up its identity. This former Roman station has yielded many archaeological finds, old milestones, paved footpaths worn down by myriads of boots, ancient woodlands and one of the most remarkable little churches in the North of England, surviving in the midst of the creeping metropolis.

This unusual walk through Adel and the Leeds district of Alwoodley visits woods made famous by the sculptor Henry Moore and the site of a large mere, transformed during the last century into Eccup Reservoir, intricate undulating paths following field boundaries with panoramic views of the city and open countryside to the north. A short detour of discovery to Adel church and the nearby open gardens at Yorkgate is recommended.

The Lawnswood Arms

A roadside cathedral to the golden age of motoring, this enormous 1920s edifice flies a mighty flag of welcome, soaring chimneys and a flash of modern signing drawing travellers in droves. Offering bright and chirpy dining from a mainly set menu, the Lawnswood Arms has a distinct appeal for families, with a 'Wacky Warehouse' play area and dishes such as burgers, filled baguettes, chicken tikka masala, steak and ale pie, steak and mushroom suet pudding, lamb shank and cod mornay. The house ales are Tetley and Calders. Opening times are 11 am to 11 pm (10.30 pm on Sundays). Telephone: 0113 267 1823.

The Walk

① Turn right from the pub and go over Holt Lane, crossing the A660 left opposite the garage and going forward down a ginnel between houses. Emerge on Holt Close and at the next junction, weave to the left, going right on a footpath at the side of the funeral directors. Continue on a gravel path between houses, going through a kissing gate onto the edge of playing fields. At the playing field corner, keep forward on a short track to Long Causeway.

② Turn left using the old paving stones and merge left with the lane at the junction, continuing to Stair Foot Lane. At this point a short detour left down Back Church Lane is recommended: see 'Places of Interest Nearby'. Go right downhill to the bottom of the lane, crossing over a stream and passing

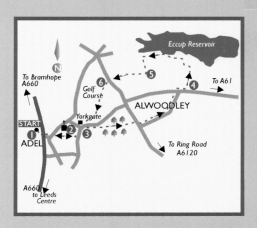

Bridge Cottage, then climb up the lane for 200 yards.

③ Turn right into a wood, passing a parking area, and go through a kissing gate into trees, following the bridleway sign. Continue forward. Make a slight detour to the left for the signposted 'Adel Crags' whose contorted rocks gave Henry Moore the inspiration for many of his sculptural forms. Swing left, passing between the playing fields and merge with an access lane, continuing to the road. Turn right past the shops for 150 yards and go left up The Avenue, continuing past the houses to the junction with Alwoodley Lane. Turn right for 200 yards.

④ Turn left opposite Mount Drive, following the public footpath sign down a pedestrian lane between a copse and a golf course, and drop down to Goodrick Lodge – Eccup Reservoir is on the right. Turn left on a track, following a public footpath sign, swinging right between a fence and a hedge. Go through a gate into a large field and go forward for 35 yards, turning left in the corner, following the

The Norman door knocker at the church in Adel

PLACES OF INTEREST NEARBY

Just a few hundred yards down Back Church Lane are two distinctly different attractions, the exquisite garden of **Yorkgate** and the famous **Adel church**. Yorkgate is an award winning horticultural masterpiece opened periodically (usually from 2 pm to 5 pm) during the summer months in aid of charities. Contact the British Red Cross on 01274 620999 for dates and opening times. Nicholas Pevsner, the celebrated architectural historian, was never one to wax lyrical about any building, his measured prose referring to Adel's church of St John the Baptist as 'one of the best and most complete Norman village churches in Yorkshire', the treasures within being described as 'memorably sumptuous' and 'of special interest'. The arched doorway and the sanctuary knocker are unforgettable. In the churchyard, near the entrance gates is an intriguing collection of stone coffins and a number of grinding wheels from the former Eccup Mill.

sign and the fence line between the wood and the reservoir. Continue for about 700 yards to the field corner and turn sharp left opposite the stile, walking along the field edge uphill to the field corner.

⑤ Cross the stile and turn right, following the yellow arrow marker fieldside, weaving left to a second stile. Cross onto the edge of a golf practice area and walk left to the lane, crossing right.

⑥ Go left, following the Meanwood Valley Trail sign alongside a golf course. Follow the weaving path through a gate and continue fieldside, dropping down and swinging right and then left to a stile. Cross and keep left through the wood to Stair Foot Lane, going right on the outward route, back to the pub.

Roundhay Park, Leeds

WATER COLOURS

The Mansion

MAP REF: OS LANDRANGER 104 (GR 331383)	WALK 11	DISTANCE: 2½ MILES

DIRECTIONS TO START: ROUNDHAY PARK IS ABOUT 4 MILES NORTH-EAST OF LEEDS CITY CENTRE. ACCESS IS SIGNPOSTED FROM THE A58 AND THE LEEDS OUTER RING ROAD (A6120). **PARKING:** PARK IN THE HOTEL CAR PARK OR ON MANSION LANE.

A former royal chase of great antiquity, Roundhay Park was purchased by the Corporation of Leeds for £139,000 and opened to the public as a recreation ground in 1872. With two beautiful lakes surrounded by formal gardens and vast swathes of lawn and woodland, the 700 acre park has been popular with visitors ever since. A miniature Windermere covering an area of 33 acres, the largest of its lakes was formed in 1815, taking its name from the battle of Waterloo.

This promenade in the grand style enjoys all the traditional attractions of a municipal park including lakeside and woodland strolls, a miniature railway, prize-winning gardens and a waterside café, with the added enjoyment of a visit to the acclaimed Tropical World – a rainforest re-creation featuring exotic plants, birds, bats, butterflies, small animals and fish. Roundhay Park is open daily from 10 am to dusk.

The Mansion

Bought along with the estate, this palatial Late Georgian building once belonged to successful London banker, Thomas Nicholson. Erected in 1826, its most arresting feature is a spectacular portico of four enormous columns supporting a pediment. Inside it is equally attractive, a spacious public bar and an elegant restaurant looking onto rose gardens. Set among the flowers and perched high above the Upper Lake with long distance views, the terrace is just the place for the warm summer months. Lunches and dinners are served daily, weekly changing menus typically including beefsteak and vegetable pie with suet crust and roast shallots, sautéed lambs kidneys with red wine and onion sauce, baked fillet of haddock with crème fraiche and gateaux of aubergine and feta cheese with a tomato and basil sauce. The house ales are John Smith's and Theakston XB and Black Bull. Bar opening times are Monday to Saturday 11 am to 11 pm. Sunday hours are 12 noon to 10.30 pm. Telephone: 0113 266 1341 and 266 3493.

The Walk

① Go left from the hotel over the car park, cross the road and keep left over the next car park, dropping down on a woodland footpath to the left of the Upper Lake. Swing right to the miniature railway track and follow the lake bank. Where the bank goes right, keep going forward into woodland and walk on to the Ivy Castle. A grand folly,

this imitation stronghold was originally fitted with stained glass and a bust of Prince Arthur.

② Turn right through the castle archway downhill onto the grassland and keep right to the top of Waterloo Lake. Follow the banks of the lake right, going left towards the newly constructed dam wall – a magnificent waterfall used to emerge here. Go right over the dam wall footway to the spillway. Turn right along the

PLACES OF INTEREST NEARBY

Tropical World has one of the largest collections of tropical plants outside Kew Gardens, its steamy jungle groves, pools and waterfalls creating realistic habitats for rare butterflies, birds and fish. Popular with children, this amazing attraction has displays of tropical fish including massive pacu and piranha, a bedimmed Nocturnal House where you can see bats, monkeys, bush babies and cavies and a Cacti House. Open every day from 10 am to 5.30 pm. There is a modest admission charge. Telephone: 0113 266 1850.

The colourful Canal Gardens in Roundhay Park

traffic-free tarmac drive to the café. Steer left over the car park away from the café and walk on to the left of the cricket pitch, uphill to the park gates.

③ Go through and cross the road, using the zebra crossing, swinging right and following a sign to the Canal Gardens through a gateway. Riotous colours, exuberant fountains and the plumage of exotic birds combine here, in what was the old kitchen garden to the Mansion House, to create one of the most attractive gardens in the North of England. Swing right, left and left again around the water feature and turn right through an archway into the National Rose Society Trial Grounds, inter-planted with rose bushes and prize-winning dahlias and violas. Turn right in front of Tropical World and exit the gardens through an arch to the main road. Cross and proceed straight forward down Mansion Lane, back to the hotel.

Stanbury

WORTHERING HEIGHTS

The Old Silent

MAP REF: OS LANDRANGER 104 (GR 003371)

WALK 12

DISTANCE: 2 MILES

DIRECTIONS TO START: THIS ISOLATED INN IS DETACHED FROM THE VILLAGE OF STANBURY (½ MILE EAST OF THE INN). STANBURY IS 1½ MILES WEST OF HAWORTH. THE EASIEST ROAD TO HAWORTH IS THE A629 FROM KEIGHLEY. **PARKING:** PARK IN THE INN CAR PARK.

Even before the celebrated Brontë sisters came to the brooding Haworth Moors, the area had a reputation for dourness and dark mystery, precipitous valleys, high moors and ubiquitous millstone grit conspiring in wild austerity. Built on a high Pennine ridge on an ancient pack-horse route between Yorkshire and Lancashire, Stanbury has a long history of farming and hand-loom weaving, a number of persecuted Quaker weavers taking refuge in the village in 1656. The Industrial Revolution brought five mills to the district, the River Worth to the north and other moorland streams providing power before locally mined coal was used to drive steam engines. Today, the village is quietness itself.

Beginning at a historic pub, this short walk visits the village and orbits a picturesque patchwork of fields in the Worth valley, the return track taking us to a restored mill by the river.

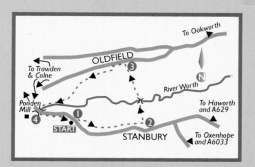

The Old Silent

With awards by the barrelful, this irresistible, stone-built gem of an inn draws customers from every continent, its increasingly famous menu having as many readers as *Wuthering Heights*. With a 400 year history that includes a resident ghost and a rumoured visit by Bonny Prince Charlie – on pain of having their tongues cut out, the locals were asked to remain silent – this atmospheric and beautifully preserved inn has won national 'Pub of the Year' awards together with accolades for its real ales ... but the real attraction is the food. Try the steak, Guinness and mushroom pie, chargrilled sausage, brandy flamed chicken breast with a cream, mushroom and spring onion sauce, moussaka, barbary duck, oak smoked gammon steak, fisherman's pie or the pan-fried salmon served with cherry tomatoes and a basil dressing. The house ales are Theakston, Old Speckled Hen and John Smith's. Opening times on Monday to Friday are 11 am to 3 pm and 5 pm to 11 pm. Saturday hours are 11 am to 11 pm. Sunday hours are 12 noon to 10.30 pm. It is advisable to book ahead for meals. Telephone: 01535 647437.

The Walk

①Turn right from the inn along the lane and go left, following a public footpath sign through a wall gap and continuing over a field wallside to a stile. Cross into a second field. Veer right to a stile and cross into a third field, following a wall down. Go through a gap into a fourth field and keep forward through a gate into the fifth field. Continue forward into the sixth field and pick up an old track (this used to be the village's main street), walking on for a further 200 yards.

②Turn left on a descending track, following a wall. Drop down across the field to a gate, going through and following a yellow arrow marker forward. Veer left to a footbridge over the River Worth. Cross and veer left to a stile. Cross and follow the yellow arrow marker on the top of a fence post, climbing up and going through a hedge gap. Keep ascending wallside and cross a stile right. Turn left, following the yellow arrow marker up and continuing on the rough track to the road and Oldfield.

③Turn left and after 200 yards, go left before the school, between the gate pillars marked 'Oldfield House 1820'. Drop down for 150 yards and swing right through the gates, following the yellow arrow markers, crossing the garden edge to a stile. Cross into a field and walk on to a second stile, crossing into a second field and going through a gate. Cross the access track to Oldfield End Farm and proceed forward through a gate into a third field. Cross a stile and continue

The Keighley and Worth Valley Railway

PLACES OF INTEREST NEARBY

The Japanese street signs tell you that Haworth is an international Mecca for Brontë fans. The centrepiece of the many Brontë attractions in the town is the **Brontë Parsonage Museum**. The lifelong home of Charlotte, Emily and Anne Brontë, the parsonage exhibits period rooms with original furnishings and personal treasures such as pictures, clothes and manuscripts. Open daily apart from Christmas and New Year and mid January to early February. Telephone: 01535 642323. Nearby is the **Black Bull** pub where the dissolute Branwell Brontë drank and consumed his opium. The **Keighley and Worth Valley Railway** runs vintage, steam-hauled trains between Keighley, Haworth and Oxenhope on a preserved branch line immortalised in the film *The Railway Children*. Operates daily in summer and every weekend. Telephone: 01535 645214/ 647777.

over a fourth field left to a stile, crossing into a fifth field. Go left to a gate opening into the sixth field. Cross, dropping down left on a track between a fence and wall for 100 yards and swing right into the seventh field, crossing a stile and weaving left to the trees. Pass a pond on the left and go left over a stile to the river. Cross a streamlet on a planked bridge and continue to the lane. On the right is one of the most famous textile mills in the North of England. Ponden Mill now sells fabrics, knitwear crafts and gifts. Visitors can eat in the Weavers Buttery. Telephone: 01535 643500.

④ Turn left over the bridge, back to the inn.

Calverley

ALONG THE LEEDS COUNTRY WAY

The Elmwood

MAP REF: OS LANDRANGER 104 (GR 212368)	WALK 13	DISTANCE: $4^1/_2$ MILES

DIRECTIONS TO START: CALVERLEY IS 7 MILES NORTH-WEST OF LEEDS CENTRE (A647 AND THEN A657). ALTERNATIVE ACCESS OFF THE LEEDS RING ROAD (A6120). **PARKING:** PARK IN THE HOTEL CAR PARK TO THE REAR.

High above a sweeping bend in the River Aire, independent Calverley jealously guards its green-belt encompassing extensive woods and fields. For over 600 years, the village depended on agriculture and the weaving of woollen goods, locally quarried millstone creating an abiding legacy of old weavers' cottages and the far grander homes of the mill-owning entrepreneurs.

This surprising walk, on parts of the Leeds Country Way and a network of tracks known as the Pudsey Parish Paths, discovers many of Calverley's oldest buildings including the parish church of St Wilfred, part of which dates from the 12th century, a now defunct mill and the restored artisans' settlement known as Woodhall Hills Hamlet. The ghost of the former Lord of the Manor, Walter Calverley, is said to haunt one ancient building – Old Hall. In April 1605 he committed a series of atrocious murders here, stabbing his wife and two sons. He was pressed to death in York in August 1605.

The Elmwood

Formerly known as Elmwood House, this elegant 19th century mansion was a Calverley wool magnate's home. Extended and converted for hotel use, the building still retains many original features, preserved fireplaces and wainscoting being particularly attractive. Outside, the hotel has an inviting terrace and an extensive beer garden. Its varied restaurant and bar menu includes roasted red pepper tart, mushroom stroganoff, chicken topped with orange pâté and wrapped in puff pastry, lamb steak with basil mash and a range of chargrilled steak dishes. The ale options are Theakston XB, Stones, Caffrey's and Worthington. Opening times Monday to Saturday are 11 am to 11 pm. Sunday hours are 12 noon to 10.30 pm. Telephone: 0113 255 8002.

The Walk

① Turn right from the rear of the hotel down the side access lane and go left and left again up Monson Avenue. After 250 yards, go right, following a footpath sign between house gardens, weaving left and right. Turn right down the lane and turn next left for 250 yards, going next right down Thornhill Street. Notice the fascinating variety of old cottages in this street. Walk on to the A657 and cross right.

② Go left at the side of the parish church down Thornhill Drive and walk on to the gate, veering right to a side gate and the Pudsey Parish Paths sign. Go through, following a yellow arrow marker fieldside to a side gate. Go through and continue to

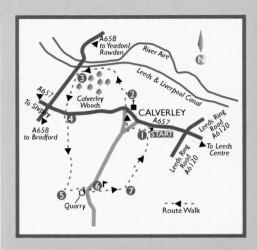

a third gate, going through and veering left, then entering the edge of Calverley Wood via a wall gap. Follow the edge of the wood forward and down for about 350 yards and veer left to a stile and a footpath marker. Turn right for 50 yards and take the left hand fork, dropping off the hillock left to merge with the broad path. At the marker stone, fork left following the blue and yellow arrow markers, arcing left and dropping downhill. Continue to the kissing gate and go through, walking on to the end of Thornhill Drive.

③ Ignoring the first path left, go straight forward and left on the broad track on the edge of West Wood. Continue uphill to the A657 and cross.

④ Keep forward on Ravenscliffe Road for about 200 yards and go left in front of the old mill for the same distance, turning right on the bend, following the marked footpath. Continue for just over a mile through Bill Wood, Round Wood and Ravenscliffe Wood.

⑤ Turn sharp left on a rough track past

The Abbey House Museum, Kirkstall

the abandoned quarry. At the quarry perimeter, turn right, following the footpath marker between the cliff and the woodland. Go left to a gate and then straight forward following the yellow arrow marker and passing through Woodhall Hills Hamlet. Notice the dated keystone of 1896.

⑥ Turn right for 130 yards and go left, following a signpost, crossing the fairway of a golf course. There are good views from here of Leeds. Follow the yellow-arrowed marker posts, cross a second fairway and proceed through a fence gap down a field edge. In the corner, keep forward through a fence gap onto a narrow path and proceed to an intersection of tracks.

⑦ Turn left on Priesthorpe Lane, passing Springwood Cottage. At the junction, go

left past Woodlands Hall and turn right, following the public bridleway sign on a walled track. Follow the track left between fields – there are surprising views from here of Hawksworth Moor – and drop down right on a sunken path to the houses, swinging right down Monson Avenue, turning right, right and left, back to the hotel.

PLACES OF INTEREST NEARBY

A little over 4 miles east is the ruined shell of **Kirkstall Abbey** and the **Abbey House Museum**. One of the most influential and powerful religious houses in the kingdom, Kirkstall was once the hub of the Yorkshire woollen trade. The Cistercian abbey was built in 1175 from millstone grit. Housed in what was the abbey gatehouse, the museum has three replica streets complete with period shops and a collection of old costumes, games and toys. Open from Tuesday to Saturday. Telephone: 0113 275 5821.

Harecroft

UNDERNEATH THE ARCHES

The Station

<table>
<tr><td>MAP REF: OS LANDRANGER 104
(GR 084356)</td><td>WALK 14</td><td>DISTANCE: 2½ MILES</td></tr>
</table>

DIRECTIONS TO START: HARECROFT IS MIDWAY BETWEEN BRADFORD AND HAWORTH ON THE B6144. **PARKING:** PARK IN THE CAR PARK OPPOSITE THE PUB.

Modern Harecroft is but a flash of cottages on a B road between the city of Bradford and the tourist town of Haworth, speeding motorists paying little heed to an engineering marvel that marked out this tiny settlement as a wonder of the railway age. At a shivering height, a magnificent 17 arch viaduct curves its way across a deep valley, huge blocks of locally quarried gritstone raising the track to a dizzy 120 feet. The track has long since been torn up and the railway station that served Harecroft and the surrounding villages of Wilsden, Denholme and Cullingworth is now a private house but, seemingly impervious to weather and the passing years, the viaduct remains.

This interesting stroll begins on Station Road, crossing over the old line towards Hewenden Reservoir and on to the viaduct itself, passing under one of its 50 ft spans. The route then follows a streamside path to Hallas Bridge, returning over field paths and tracks, back to the pub.

The Station

The simple but homely Station lost its passengers when the line closed. Now a popular locals' pub comprising three separate, comfortably furnished rooms, it typically offers traditional staple meals such as giant Yorkshire puddings, Cumberland sausage, shepherd's pie and various filled baguettes, together with its locally famous home-made speciality, stuffed pancakes. The ale tally is Theakston, Timothy Taylor and Cumberland ales. The pub has a small beer garden to the rear. Opening hours on Monday to Friday are 3 pm to 11 pm. For the rest of the week the hours are 12 noon to 11 pm (10.30 pm on Sundays). Telephone: 01535 272430.

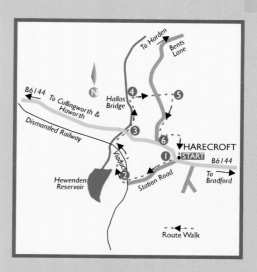

The Walk

① Cross the road from the pub, going diagonally right down Station Road. Follow the road as it peters out and curves right and pass by the old railway station, crossing the cutting on a bridge. Keep forward and go through a kissing gate. Hewenden Reservoir comes into view.

② Drop down right on a path towards the viaduct and swing right under one of the arches, going left on a track between dry stone walls to the beck. Swing right, following the beck up on a path to the road.

③ Cross the road (with care – poor sight lines) going right for 50 yards and turn left, following a public footpath sign through a wall gap. Follow the yellow arrow marker right and arc left through a wall gap. Keep going forward, following the beck up, and weave left and down, going through a wall gap. Go right on the access road to the mill at Hallas Bridge.

④ Turn right, following the footpath to Bents Lane, walking straight on uphill and crossing the lane. Go through a wall gap and climb steeply, going through a wall gap to the track known as Nab Lane.

⑤ Turn right down the track and

PLACES OF INTEREST NEARBY

Nearby Bradford has a number of prestige attractions including the **National Museum of Photography, Film and Television**. Six floors of interactive displays and exhibits chart the multi-faceted history of the media. Free entry. Open all year, Tuesdays to Sundays (and Bank Holiday Mondays.) Telephone: 01274 202030. Dedicated to the history, development and technology of colour, Bradford's unusual and eye-catching **Colour Museum** is unique in Europe. Open Tuesday to Saturday. Telephone: 01274 390955.

The Hewenden viaduct keeps watch over the reservoir

continue forward and down, merging right with Bents Lane. Continue forward towards the road. Just before the junction, turn left, following a public footpath sign through a gate.

⑥ Follow the path up, keeping to the right of the old quarry and cross a stile, going left along the quarry top. After 100 yards, swing right and go left through a wall opening and right wallside. Swing right and after 150 yards go through a gap by the gate entrance. Turn right down the lane, back to the inn.

Leeds

CITY SLICKING

Whitelocks

MAP REF: OS LANDRANGER 104 (GR 303335)

WALK 15

DISTANCE: 2 MILES

DIRECTIONS TO START: WHITELOCKS IS IN TURK'S HEAD YARD OFF BRIGGATE (NEAR MARKS AND SPENCER), LEEDS. **PARKING:** LEEDS CITY CENTRE IS BECOMING INCREASINGLY PEDESTRIANISED AND PARKING IS AT A PREMIUM AND EXPENSIVE ALTHOUGH ON STREET 'PAY AND DISPLAY' AND MULTI-STOREY FACILITIES ARE AVAILABLE NEARBY.

As befits the largest and most commercially successful city in Yorkshire, Leeds has some fine architecture, its monumental town hall of 1858 setting the grandest scene, handsome squares, lavishly adorned former warehouses and hundreds of designer shops adding to an experience that can include visits to the City Museum, the City Art Gallery, the Royal Armouries Museum, the famous City Varieties and the Yorkshire Playhouse.

This exciting pavements and pedestrian precincts stroll is packed with interest. The renaissance of Leeds as a leading commercial, legal, cultural and residential centre has breathed new life into a city founded on agriculture, heavy engineering and wool; links with its past include the remarkable Corn Exchange, typically built like other public buildings in millstone grit.

Whitelocks

Imagine, if you will, an Edwardian gentleman's narrow boat marooned and roofed over in a creek of a great city. Fit it out with tiles, brasswork, a copper-sheathed bar, etched and stained glass and long mirrors and install a sprinkling of tables. Invest your craft with real ale, a bevy of aproned serving maids and the most potent nasal allurement known to man. Now, follow the tantalising aroma of roast beef and Yorkshire puddings down the alley. Congratulations! You've discovered one of the most timeless and remarkable pubs in the North of England – Whitelocks First City Luncheon Bar. Reputation is sign enough for this licensed institution first founded as the Turk's Head in 1715, its modern name deriving from a more recent family who held the licence for 90 years. Hardly touched since its last make-over in 1886, Whitelocks serves ever popular traditional staples such as rare beef sandwiches with an assortment of pickles, meat pie, roast potatoes and mushy peas, lamb chops and seafood pie. The house ales are McEwan 80/-, Ruddles, Theakston, Old Speckled Hen and John Smith's Smooth. Opening times Monday to Saturday are 11 am to 11 pm. Sunday hours are 12 noon to 10.30 pm. Telephone: 0113 245 3950.

The Walk

① Turn right down the alley into Briggate and go left past the Harvey Nichols store. After 300 yards turn right into the Victoria

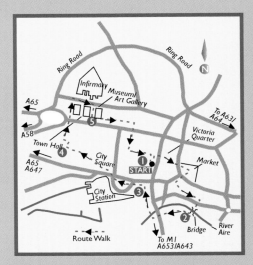

Quarter (this sumptuous mall is covered with a dazzling stained glass roof). Exit onto Vicar Lane, go right, cross the road left and enter the Leeds City Markets building. Leave the markets and exit on Kirkgate, going forward on Call Lane to the Corn Exchange. Opened in 1863, this oval building was a trading centre for grain. It now houses speciality shops. Turn left up Crown Street, swinging right and going next left on Assembly Street under the railway arch, swinging left and right. Cross the road left down The Calls and turn right on a new pedestrian bridge over the River Aire. The large building along the riverbank to the left is the Royal Armouries Museum.

② Turn right down Dock Street and turn right again on Bridge End over Leeds Bridge. The original medieval crossing had a bridge chapel. This structure was a subject for the first ever moving pictures. Cross the road and continue along Briggate.

③ Turn left along Boar Lane and continue

Dazzling stained glass illuminates the Victorian Quarter in Leeds

PLACES OF INTEREST NEARBY

Perhaps the most unusual of the many attractions in Leeds is the **Thackray Medical Museum**, just 2 miles north-east of the city centre, on Beckett Street. This highly interactive museum charts the history of medicine and health in the city in a series of tableaux and reconstructions. 'Pain, Pus and Blood' tells the dramatic story of surgery. Got the flavour? Not for the faint hearted! Opening times Tuesdays to Sundays and Bank Holiday Mondays are 10 am to 5 pm. Telephone: 0113 245 7084.

into City Square. Pass in front of the Majestic Hotel (the traffic island in the middle of the square is dominated by a recurring Leeds icon – an equestrian statue of the Black Prince). Turn right across the road opposite the railway station entrance and go left down Quebec Street, crossing the next junction and going straight forward along Park Place.

④ Turn right on Central Street and go next left down St Paul's Street. The highly distinctive and decorative building on your right is a Moorish and Mohammedan crested showpiece originally built in 1878 as a warehouse for Leeds' first clothing manufacturer John Barran. Turn right on Park Square West to Westgate. The terrific Town Hall is in front. An instantly recognisable building, it has become a symbol of local government in England. Cross and go left up Park Street, turning right on Great George Street. Swing right and left behind the Town Hall and turn right on Calverley Street.

⑤ Turn left over the piazza in front of the Art Gallery, pass the war memorial and cross into The Headrow, walking uphill. Go next right down Albion Street and drop downhill. Turn left into the pedestrian precinct on Albion Place, passing lines of shops, back to Briggate. Go right and right again to return to the pub.

Ledsham

CHASE TO CHEENY BASIN

The Chequers

MAP REF: OS LANDRANGER 105 (GR 455298)	WALK 16	DISTANCE: 4½ MILES

DIRECTIONS TO START: NORTH OF CASTLEFORD, LEDSHAM IS ONE MILE WEST OF THE
A1/A63 JUNCTION AT SELBY FORK. **PARKING:** PARK IN THE PUB CAR PARK

The highway planners who designed West Yorkshire's network of roads must have been incorrigible scribblers at school such is the tangle of concrete hereabouts. Ledsham is boxed in on all sides by arterial routes but its leafy dells defend the silence well, not even a distant rumble disturbing one of the prettiest villages in the county.

This linear walk takes us through Ledston Park, a hunting chase of the nearby Elizabethan mansion of Ledston Hall, along forest and field tracks to the former coal mining settlement of Ledston Luck. Our destination lies across the Roman road known as Ermine Street at the hilltop village of Kippax. With tremendous views of the Aire valley and beyond south to the wilds of Derbyshire, Kippax is built around its Norman church of St Mary, an adjacent hillock marking the Scheduled Ancient Monument Site of a motte and bailey castle known locally for centuries as Cheeny Basin.

The Chequers

The incomparable setting, the ivied gable, the excellent food, the cosy interior where you can kick off your boots and banter, the real ale to quaff by the pintful and the beer garden smothered in summer flowers. This is a yardstick, a definition of the classical English pub that knocks modern imitations of licensed premises for six! Low beamed and intimate with log fires during the winter months, the Chequers offers a largely traditional menu that members of the redoubtable Pickwick Club would drool on – roast beef, Yorkshire ham, Cumberland sausage, mushroom and bacon tart, steak and mushroom pie and smoked haddock fish pie rounded off by steamed sponge pudding. Pass the negus! Standard meals and daily specials are available either in the bars or, at weekends, in the upstairs Hastings Restaurant. The choice of ales is Theakston, John Smith's and the locally brewed Brown Cow. Opening times Monday to Saturday are 11 am to 11 pm. The pub is closed on Sundays. Telephone: 01977 683135.

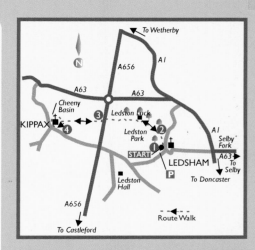

The Walk

① Go left from the car park on the bend and fork right opposite the pub on Park Lane. Continue past the houses and merge with a track swinging left into a wood.

② At the fork, go left following the footpath sign, climbing up and swinging right by the edge of the wood. Swing left at the field corner, go right through a gate gap and follow a woodside hedge path, arcing left away from the wood. Walk on for 100 yards left of the farm and turn right, following a yellow arrow marker over a stile. Veer left over a sparsely planted copse for 30 yards and cross a second stile, keeping forward alongside a farm wall. Fork right at the end of the wall, passing in front of the farmhouse and walk up to a yellow-tipped marker post. Go left,

PLACES OF INTEREST NEARBY

Opposite the pub is a very special **Saxon church**. Much of All Saints' was erected 1,200 years ago, making it the oldest standing building in West Yorkshire. A leaflet available in the church explains the architectural features. A booklet about the life of the remarkable but little known Lady Betty Hastings can also be purchased. The daughter of the 7th Earl of Huntingdon, she inherited a fortune and nearby Ledstone Hall in 1705, devoting her life to charitable and educational works. She founded the orphanage east of the church in 1721, creating a number of trusts that still survive today.

All Saints church Ledsham dates from Saxon times

following the arrow marker, and continue along the woodland edge. Swing left to cross a planked bridge over a ditch and swing right, following the woodland edge left on an arc. Swing right on the well-defined path into the next field and follow the path up to the road. The site of Ledston Luck Colliery (now an Enterprise Park) and its satellite village is to the right.

③ Turn left along the A656 for 300 yards. On your left is an old milestone. Turn right across the road and continue straight forward on a tarmac field-edge path towards Kippax, heading for the church tower. Swing left into Kippax and go right on Sandgate Terrace past the allotments. Cross the road and proceed forward on the footway between the school grounds and pass the cemetery, going left by its fence and right into St Mary's churchyard. The largely complete Norman church is characterised by the excessive use of herringbone masonry.

④ Take a clockwise circuit of the church (go left through the second gate to Cheeny Basin) and return to the pub by the outward route.

Tong

A TRAIL TWIXT TWO CITIES

The Greyhound

MAP REF: OS LANDRANGER 104 (GR 223307)	**WALK 17**	DISTANCE: $4^1/_2$ MILES

DIRECTIONS TO START: TONG IS MIDWAY BETWEEN BRADFORD AND LEEDS. IT IS BEST REACHED FROM JUNCTION 27 OF THE M62, GOING NORTH-WEST FOR JUST OVER 2 MILES ON THE A650 AND TURNING RIGHT ON A MINOR ROAD FOR A FURTHER MILE. **PARKING:** PARK IN THE INN CAR PARK.

Deep encircling valleys have contrived a happy isolation for this highly attractive place. Tong has an imposing 18th century church, a brick-built hall of 1702 and a number of listed stone cottages, the harmonious ensemble enclosing a scene that is the essence of olde England. Cricket pitches and time-worn inns go together like ham and eggs and good beer, both English staples being regularly served by the Greyhound within a bounce of the boundary line.

This route explores the unspoilt and strangely quiet countryside between the twin cities – I came in July and never saw a soul – following an intriguing network of long abandoned pack-horse trails, some beckside, many paved with flagstones. Very steep in places, the track takes you to Black Carr Wood, seeing, on the return leg, something of the skill of our railway pioneers in the remains of a dismantled railway. Two additional pubs are passed along the way.

The Greyhound

This appealing little inn has no windows on the batsman's side, its largely unaltered low interior housing a period bar decorated with a handsome collection of Toby jugs and rustic prints. The Greyhound serves a cosmopolitan collection of dishes such as Cajun chicken breasts, chicken korma, beef stroganoff, poached haddock and sirloin steak, as well as the traditional ham alongside meat and potato pie and fish and chips. The house ales are Tetley and Calders and a regularly changed guest beer. Opening times are 11.30 am to 11 pm on Monday to Saturday. Sunday hours are 12 noon to 10.30 pm. Telephone: 0113 285 2427.

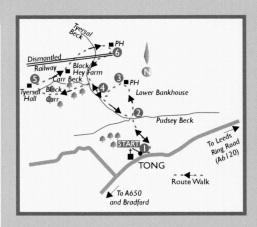

The Walk

① Turn left from the inn on the footway and pass the preserved pinfold and the water pump. Turn left again down Keeper Lane, following the public bridleway. Go through a gate and follow the blue arrow marker downhill. Drop down to the bottom on the causeway, weave right and cross the Pudsey Beck on a footbridge, going left to a marker post.

② Go straight forward, following the direction sign to Fulneck, climbing steeply uphill. Go left past the cottages numbered 25 and 26 on Lower Bankhouse and climb up to the Bankhouse Inn.

③ Swing left downhill – Scholebrook Lane – following the public bridleway. Take the left fork at the cattery/kennels and drop down to the Leeds Country Way sign 40 yards before the bridge.

④ Turn right through the upright posts, following the weaving path beckside. After about 500 yards, look out for a bridge on the left and veer left, crossing the bridge into Black Carr Wood. Go through a gate and follow the path left, walking on for just over ½ mile. Where the wood narrows to a point – about 400 yards before the end of the trees – look out for a right hand fork, following this fork above the Carr Beck and crossing the water right on the long stones and mounting the steps. Cross the stile and follow the yellow arrow marker at the edge of a field, walking up at the side of the barn to a lane. Just left along the lane is Tyersal Hall. A fascinating assortment of variously figured stones in situ adorn its boundary wall.

⑤ Turn right down the lane and gradually merge with the line of the abandoned railway to the left. Pass Black Hey Farm and steer left between the massive bridge abutments. Drop down into the wood and cross the Tyersal Beck on a bridge, climbing up a bank and going through a gate. Go through a gate gap and walk on, passing the Fox and Grapes pub.

The parish pump, Tong

PLACES OF INTEREST NEARBY

A short distance from the village, not far from the A650 junction, is a large garden centre stocking a wide range of plants, trees, garden furniture, equipment, fountains, seeds and other sundries. **Tong Garden Centre** is open every day.

Bowling Hall off the A650 is one of the oldest and most interesting buildings in Bradford. Once the centre of an extensive estate, it has been preserved, housing period furniture and local history bygones. Open Bank Holiday Mondays and daily Wednesday to Sunday. Telephone: 01274 723057.

marker through a gap in the wall, then walking alongside the stream to join the outward route.

⑥ Turn right on an unsigned rough track, dropping down on a causeway, crossing the railway cutting on a bridge. Weave downhill and take the left hand fork. Just before you come to the stream in the bottom go left, following a yellow arrow

⑦ Instead of retracing your steps left uphill, go right and just before the footbridge go left between two upright stones and cross a stile, following the footpath marker. At the edge of the golf course keep forward and go through a fence gap, following the beck back to the Fulneck sign, retracing your steps back to the inn.

Wainstalls

WIND SOME

The Withens Hotel

MAP REF: OS LANDRANGER 104 (GR 045306)	WALK 18	DISTANCE: 4½ MILES

DIRECTIONS TO START: WAINSTALLS IS 2¾ MILES NORTH-WEST OF HALIFAX. TAKE PELLON LANE FROM HALIFAX CENTRE AND FOLLOW THE STEADILY CLIMBING ROAD TO WAINSTALLS, FORKING RIGHT OUT OF THE VILLAGE AT THE DELVERS PUB FOR A FURTHER 1½ MILES. **PARKING:** PARK IN THE PUB CAR PARK.

Wainstalls is only the postal address and base camp for this epic West Yorkshire summit walk whose panoramic views take in most of the county. On an ancient pack-horse route between Keighley and Halifax, Wainstalls developed as a community sustained by farming, weaving and delving (the local term for quarrying stone), while the construction of quarries and reservoirs drew vast numbers of labourers to the area during the 19th century. The bracing airs of this lofty place have been used to good effect in recent years, 23 wind turbines dominating the skyline. They generate enough power to supply the annual electricity needs of 7,500 homes but arouse much controversy. To me though, these synchronised acrobats are utterly benign, making no more noise than the gentle swish of my map case.

The Withens Hotel

At 1,392 feet above sea level, the Withens is the highest inn in West Yorkshire. Built in 1862, with yard thick walls and a gable end sign that winks out a welcome through the swirling mist in winter, this inn is not so much a casual halt but a life-saver, roaring fires and home-cooked, hearty meals adding to the euphoria of steaming socks. But beware the resident ghost of a lonely traveller! In summer though, the pub is transformed, seeing more boots than a regiment of foot, walking parties, mountain bikers and horse riders all converging on its doors. The Withens has an added attraction for families, an adjacent 'petting farm' giving youngsters the opportunity of handling rare breed chickens, rabbits, guinea pigs, ducks and other docile animals. The pub menu includes farmhouse grills, a range of steak dishes, roast lunches, curries and sandwiches, the 'home-made' tag even extending to the hand-chopped chips. You can select from an impressive line up of real ales – Timothy Taylor, Withens Rambler, Tetley and Black Sheep. The opening times are Tuesday to Friday 12 noon to 3 pm and 7 pm to 11 pm. Weekend openings are 12 noon to 11 pm (10.30 pm on Sundays) (restricted Saturday hours in winter are 12 noon to 3 pm and 7 pm to 11 pm). Telephone: 01422 244809.

The Walk

① Turn left from the pub and go through a gate onto the moor, for 350 yards.

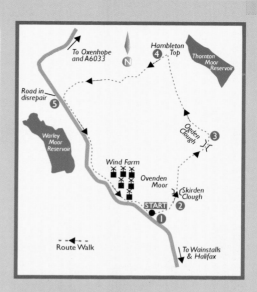

② Turn left, following a footpath sign. Drop down and cross Skirden Clough on the concrete bridge, swinging left and right (there is a view of Ogden Reservoir on the right) on a well-defined path to a cairn. Continue following the path right and drop down to a stile, crossing right at the edge of Ogden Clough. Drop down left on steps to the spillway and cross right, going left up the steps.

PLACES OF INTEREST NEARBY

The **Piece Hall** in Halifax is a stunning architectural gem built in the 18th century as a grand cloth hall. It now houses an art gallery, specialist shops and an outdoor market. Adjacent to the Piece Hall is the **Calderdale Industrial Museum** which presents the history of local industry in lively exhibits and machinery demonstrations. Open Tuesday to Saturday. Telephone: 01422 358087. Also in Halifax is **Eureka!**, a remarkable interactive museum designed to stimulate discovery and imagination in children aged between 3 and 12. Open daily. Telephone: 01422 330012.

Wind turbines dominate the skyline of Ovenden Moor

③ Follow the edge of the clough left and fork off right away from the clough, following the well-defined path, passing a cairn (Thornton Moor Reservoir comes into view on the right). Continue to Hambleton Top and a kissing gate on the left.

④ Turn left through the gate. Weave left through the old spoil heaps and left across Little Clough, continuing and going down left to the next clough. Swing right and walk on to what appears to be a massive cairn. On closer inspection this turns out to be a circular stone shelter. Weave left down a sunken track and walk towards Warley Moor Reservoir in the distance. Cross a stile to Cold Edge Road.

⑤ Turn left along the road (in disrepair for most of its length – see the indecipherable milestone on the left) passing the wind farm, back to the pub.

Chiserley

MOREISH

The Hare and Hounds

MAP REF: OS LANDRANGER 104 (GR 006281)	WALK 19	DISTANCE: 2 MILES

DIRECTIONS TO START: PERCHED AT A HEIGHT OF OVER 1,000 FEET, AROUND 8 MILES NORTH-WEST OF HALIFAX, CHISERLEY CAN BE REACHED FROM EITHER MYTHOLMROYD OR HEBDEN BRIDGE OFF THE A646 OR THE A6033 BUT BOTH MINOR ACCESS ROADS ARE PRECIPITOUS AND NARROW WITH ONE OR MORE HAIRPIN BENDS. **PARKING:** PARK IN THE PUB CAR PARK.

The industrial gold rush claimed every flat yard of the Calder valley within a few short years, successive settlements progressively climbing the hills in search of mill space and the power of mountain streams. At the edge of Wadsworth Moor, Chiserley is one such place, sweating mule trains and a harsh upland climate proving no obstacle to the drive of commerce. Chiserley still has its mill, a cluster of old cottages and a sizeable expansion of new houses, walkers congregating here at weekends to explore the featureless Wadsworth, Midgley and Warley Moors to the north and east.

Never leaving sight of the Hare and Hounds, this short circular foray to the edge of Wadsworth Moor on pack-horse trails and heather-bounded tracks, gives you just a sniff of desolation without any fear of getting lost. Terrific views take in the monument on Stoodley Pike and the crowded valley occupied by Mytholmroyd, Sowerby Bridge and Halifax to the south-east.

The Hare and Hounds

Sited on a former pack-horse trail, the Hare and Hounds has been a succour for travellers for centuries and it still offers the warmest of welcomes, its erstwhile stabling now providing bed and breakfast accommodation. Sturdily built, with log fires during the winter months, it has a girding menu of old favourites like Yorkshire puddings with onion gravy, tuna pasta bake, cod fish cakes, a range of steaks, Cumberland sausage, steak and mushroom and meat and potato pies and chicken tikka masala. The Hare and Hounds is a Timothy Taylor house serving the famous award-winning Landlord and Golden Best ales. With little passing trade the pub is only open in the evenings on weekdays, from 7 pm to 11 pm. Weekend opening times are 11 am (12 noon on Sundays) to 11 pm (10.30 pm on Sundays). Telephone: 01422 842671.

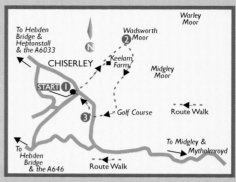

The Walk

NB: For ease of access and to enjoy the wonderful views, this walk is best reserved for fine days.

① Turn left from the pub to the junction and cross the end of Billy Lane, going straight forward on a track. Swing left at the entrance to Keelam Farm and swing right off the track, crossing a stile. Continue climbing between broken walls, cross a second stile and keep ascending wallside. Cross a further stile and weave left, going through a gate onto the moor.

② Turn right to a marker sign and follow the yellow arrow marker, arcing right,

A desirable address in Chiserley!

The view from the pub, with Stoodley Pike in the distance on the left

following the moor edge. Follow the wall down to a stile. Cross and keep forward, crossing a further stile and going left, following a yellow arrow marker. Follow the broken wall down and after 300 yards, weave left, crossing a meadow and heading for Stoodley Pike. Swing right to a third stile and before the golf course perimeter, turn right, crossing a fourth stile, following an arrow marker and dropping down to the lane.

③ Turn right on the lane, back to the pub.

PLACES OF INTEREST NEARBY

West of Chiserley, across the deep valley of the Hebden Water, is the elevated neighbouring village of **Heptonstall**. This captivating place has a notable churchyard (reputably 100,000 bodies are buried here together with the corpse of David Hartley – see Walk 21), Wesley's octagonal chapel of 1764 and a grammar school dated 1642.

North along the valley is the National Trust beauty spot of **Hardcastle Crags**.

Todmorden

SWITCHBACKS AND SHEER DROPS

The Staff of Life

<table>
<tr><td>MAP REF: OS LANDRANGER 103
(GR 916257)</td><td>WALK 20</td><td>DISTANCE: 2$\frac{1}{2}$ MILES</td></tr>
</table>

DIRECTIONS TO START: THE INN IS 1$\frac{1}{2}$ MILES NORTH-WEST OF TODMORDEN TOWN CENTRE ON THE A646 BURNLEY ROAD. **PARKING:** NO PARKING OUTSIDE THE INN. SIGNPOSTED INN CAR PARK 150 YARDS SOUTH-EAST.

At the spoke of three valleys with a plentiful supply of water, Todmorden developed as a centre for the textile trade, the damp atmosphere proving ideal for the spinning of cotton. Workers' rights campaigner John Fielden MP, who operated a model factory in the town, was responsible for large-scale industrialisation during the 1820s and 30s, his family going on to build the Unitarian Chapel and the Town Hall, the Yorkshire/Lancashire boundary running through its middle! This anomaly was rectified in 1888, Todmorden flying the white rose flag to this day.

This walk begins in what is essentially a mountain pass, the Burnley road, which snakes up the valley of the Calder between high cliffs to the old mill town of Cornholme and the industrial heartland of Lancashire to the north-west. Up steep slopes, we ascend to the hamlet of Shore, descending on a remarkable packhorse trail of switchbacks and sheer drops. Within living memory it was used by the local milk man!

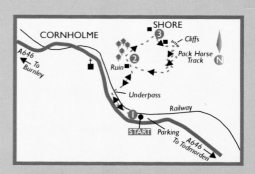

The Staff of Life

Architecturally, this is one of the most unusual inns you will come across, its three storeys looking insignificant and almost anonymous under frowning crags that cast their shadows even on the brightest days. But this is a drinking den that needs no sun, a nest of small rooms eyed by a zoological assortment of stuffed animals, guns, tools and other paraphernalia incorporating an arched cave that used to be the beer cellar. The intimate atmosphere is further enhanced by open fires on cold days and a sparkling fish tank. Heading the list of substantial meals is the range of speciality pan-fried steaks, other popular dishes including steak and kidney pie, chicken and mushroom pie, beef in Guinness, macaroni bake and stir fries. Bar top, you can choose from Timothy Taylor Landlord, Golden Best and Ram Tam and Boddingtons. Opening times on Monday to Friday are 7 pm to 11 pm. Saturday hours are 12 noon to 11 pm. On Sundays the inn is open from 12 noon to 4 pm and 7 pm to 10.30 pm. Telephone: 01706 812929.

The Walk

① Turn right from the inn along the footway and turn right on Dundee Road under the railway line, following a public footpath sign. Swing left and go through the gate to Dundee Farm, swinging right to a second gate. Go through, following the yellow arrow marker right. Weave left and walk up to the direction markers, forking right, following the yellow arrow marker. Continue past the ruin and keep generally forward, heading for the topside of the wood. Follow the line of a broken wall and cross a stile, keeping forward and crossing a second stile at the wood edge.

② Weave right and cross a further stile, heading steeply uphill, following an embankment upwards and weaving left, heading for the middle of farm buildings

In the Calder valley

Cornholme seen from the track below Shore

to a yellow arrow marker. Cross a stile and swing right on a walled track. After 150 yards go left over a stile and walk up to cross a further stile.

③ Turn right on an access track and swing left and right by the cottages, going through a courtyard and a gate onto the moor top. Pass the communications tower and cross a stile and swing left on the old packhorse track. There are stupendous views to the left but beware of the precipice! Follow this track on its hairpin descent towards the bottom of the valley and follow an arrow marker right, back to the ruin. Retrace your steps back to the inn.

PLACES OF INTEREST NEARBY

The **Todmorden Craft Centre**, situated in an attractive setting near the Rochdale Canal, has a variety of stalls and workshops and a tea shop. Open ever day but Tuesdays. Telephone: 01706 818170.

Mytholmroyd

DEEP INTO COINERS' COUNTRY

The Shoulder of Mutton

MAP REF: OS LANDRANGER 104 (GR 013258)	**WALK 21**	DISTANCE: $3\frac{1}{2}$ MILES

DIRECTIONS TO START: MYTHOLMROYD IS IN THE CALDER VALLEY, 5 MILES WEST OF HALIFAX ON THE A646. THE PUB IS SOUTH OF THE MAIN ROAD, OVER THE RIVER BRIDGE ON THE B6138, OPPOSITE THE RAILWAY STATION. **PARKING:** PARK IN THE PUB CAR PARK TO THE REAR.

Mytholmroyd, in the congested valley of the Calder, is a typically bluff Pennine town. With stone, sinew and not a little ingenuity, such historic places helped spawn the Industrial Revolution, Mytholmroyd's long history of textile manufacture surviving in a fascinating legacy of old mills, weavers' cottages and a network of packhorse routes across the hills. This adaptable and still busy town stands at the head of Cragg Vale, a once notorious centre for the counterfeiting of coins in the 1760s. The value of the local currency was so debased by the actions of a 70-strong band under the leadership of David Hartley that the Government was forced to act, the murder of an exciseman leading to the arrest of the coiners' leader. 'King David', as he was known, was hanged in York in 1770. His body lies in Heptonstall church above Hebden Bridge.

Following the river for a short distance, this leisurely stroll climbs the valley sides, using time-worn tracks smothered in bilberry and heather, the return loop taking us deep into coiners' country.

The Shoulder of Mutton

Guarding the snaking road to Cragg Vale, this appealing inn, which has an intriguing collection of coiners' tools, dies and memorabilia, is conveniently situated, the cluster of buildings on its corner including the railway station and a new Catholic church. With a big reputation for home-cooked food and regular endorsements by successive editions of CAMRA's *Good Pub Food*, the Shoulder of Mutton is deservedly popular with locals and visitors alike, serving beef in ale pie, steak and onion pie, Cumberland sausage, filled Yorkshire puddings, various roasts from the carvery and specials such as lamb's liver and onions. A large dining room is available. The house ales are Black Sheep, Flowers IPA, Marston's Pedigree, Castle Eden and Boddingtons. Opening times Monday to Friday are 11.30 am to 3 pm and 7 pm to 11 pm. Weekend hours are 11.30 am (12 noon Sundays) to 11 pm (10.30 pm on Sundays). Telephone: 01422 883165.

The Walk

① Take the signed public footpath opposite the pub, going forward alongside the Good Shepherd church, and cross the church car park, weaving right. Pass the cricket pitch and go through a gap by a gate. Swing left and right onto a broad track, walking through a linear wood that runs parallel with the railway line. Go through a gap barrier, continuing and going through a second gap barrier, and follow the fence round right and left. Swing left across the railway

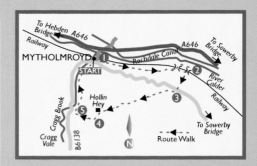

on a bridge and pass the large mill building with a date stone of 1873, walking on to the lane.

② Turn right uphill on Mill Hill and re-cross the railway on the bridge. Follow the lane left and take the track straight up, passing the stone gate pillar marked 'Little Scout Farm'. Keep forward, going up the steps. Continue through a wicket gate and follow a field wallside. Go through a gate gap and follow a wall for half its distance. Then switch to the other side of the wall, going left and immediately right, following the remaining wall up and through a wall gap to the lane.

③ Turn right and take the second of the marked footpaths, going off diagonally left, following the yellow arrow marker over a stile. Follow the wall down. Go

PLACES OF INTEREST NEARBY

Two miles north-west of Mytholmroyd along the A646 is **Hebden Bridge**, a lively and interesting town with good shops, pubs and restaurants. **Calder Valley Cruising** run horse-drawn and motorboat cruises from the marina, Easter to Christmas. Pre-booking advisable. Telephone: 01422 845557.

The new boundary stone at Mytholmroyd

through a gate gap. Keep forward, veering left, and climb steadily up. Go through a wall gap to the right of a gate and follow a wall down to a stile. Cross, walk fieldside and go through a further wall gap, keeping to the field edge. At the field corner, go through a broken wall gap right on a track, weaving left to the steps. Go left down the steps and weave right to the footpath sign. Follow the footpath sign forward to 'Hollin Hey Bank' through a gate gap, accompanying the wall round left. Weave right to a sunken track. Follow this down into the trees (the overgrown tangle tends to deflect you to the right) and swing left, continuing towards the barn, following the yellow footpath marker. Keep forward here, ignoring the yellow arrow marker off left, and continue on a track swinging right to Hollin Hey Farm. Go left by the farm buildings for 150 yards on a path between walls.

④ Turn right, following a yellow arrow marker through a wall gap, then following a walled track down over two stiles to a new farm access road. Cross and go right to find a yellow arrow marker to the right of the cottage and go left, following the marker through a fence gap, walking on to a kissing gate.

⑤ Turn right (do not go through) and follow the valley of the Cragg Brook. Follow the new access road left to a wicket gate and go through into the wood. Swing right and continue on the woodland edge path, merging with Stubbings Close. Drop down and go left on New Road, back to the pub.

Lumbutts

A HIKE TO THE PIKE

The Top Brink

MAP REF: OS LANDRANGER 103 (GR 957235)	**WALK 22**	DISTANCE: 3 MILES

DIRECTIONS TO START: THE HAMLET OF LUMBUTTS IS 2 MILES SOUTH-EAST OF TODMORDEN AND THE A646/A6033. ACCESS IS VIA STEEP AND NARROW MINOR ROADS. TAKE EITHER WOODHOUSE ROAD AT CASTLE STREET EAST OF TODMORDEN (OFF A646), OR LUMBUTTS ROAD AT KNOWL WOOD JUST SOUTH OF TODMORDEN (OFF A6033). **PARKING:** PARK IN THE INN CAR PARK.

In Lumbutts, and elsewhere in this Pennine crucible of enterprise and innovation, began an economic revolution that shook the world, the seed of the newly instituted factory system and the concept of industrialisation taking root here. In the 18th century, a frenzy of mechanisation using water-powered mills completely altered the cotton industry and the local landscape. Lumbutts had one of the most ingeniously engineered mills in the country, a system of dams serving three 30 ft diameter water wheels geared in tandem and raised one above the other in a still-surviving 104 ft high tower.

This simple but strenuous walk has a heroic destination, the martial pull of the monument on Stoodley Pike urging us ever upwards. Returning to Lumbutts, we detour by the much older settlement of Mankinholes whose old cottages were once the homes of hand-loom weavers.

The Top Brink

In nearly two decades of writing walking books, I have visited more licensed premises than a brewer's dray. This exceptional pub, in its matchless setting opposite the old mill tower and within striking distance of Stoodley Pike, should be a yardstick for all the rest. Originally built in the mid 18th century as an alehouse for Irish navvies, the Top Brink has been altered out of all recognition in recent years, serving walkers on the Pennine and Calderdale Ways and car-borne customers for the whole of the north-west of England. Flower-smothered in summer and with log fires for the winter months, this large pub is crammed with interesting treasures – sparkling brasses, antique photographs and pictures, tools and stuffed animals, the attention to detail echoing loudly in an extensive menu where everything is home-made. Try the kiln-smoked trout, the own recipe Cumberland sausage, the steak and lambs kidney pie, the fillet of beef stroganoff or the rib-eye steaks. The ale choices are Timothy Taylor, Boddingtons and Castle Eden. Opening times on Monday to Friday are 6 pm to 11 pm. Saturday hours are 12 noon to 2.30 pm and 6 pm to 11 pm. Sunday opening is 12 noon to 10.30 pm. Telephone: 01706 812696.

The Walk

① Turn left from the inn and go immediately left through a wall gap to follow a wall down, crossing a stile. Weave left pass the Youth Hostel (this was

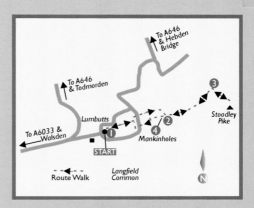

Mankinholes Hall – part of it was the workhouse, some children being employed at Lumbutts Mill). Head straight towards Stoodley Pike, weaving right and left on a track. Pass Spencer House. Go right at the entrance to Broad Carr Farm entrance.

Lumbutts Mill

Stoodley Pike

② Turn left over a stile, continuing towards the pike on a path. Keep going forward and continue past the second farmhouse to a stile.

③ Opposite this stile, turn right and walk up the steep hillside to Stoodley Pike. This structure was erected in 1856 to commemorate peace after the Napoleonic Wars. Retrace your steps to point 2.

④ Keep straight on here and proceed between walls, walking into Mankinholes. Turn right to the Youth Hostel and turn left on the outward route, back to the inn.

PLACES OF INTEREST NEARBY

Nearby **Todmorden** has a good mixture of shops, galleries and museums. The **Todmorden Toy and Model Museum** is open from Wednesday to Saturday. Telephone: 01706 818365/813033. Saunter along the towpath of the **Rochdale Canal** to rekindle the joy of level walking!

Walsden

TWO LOCKS, ONE CLOUGH AND A BOWL OF STEAMING TRIPE

The Waggon and Horses

MAP REF: OS LANDRANGER 103
(GR 935214)

WALK 23

DISTANCE: 2 MILES

DIRECTIONS TO START: WALSDEN IS 2 MILES SOUTH OF TODMORDEN ON THE A6033.
PARKING: USE THE CAR PARK OPPOSITE THE PUB.

Set in the gorge of a glacial valley, Walsden was primarily a clothing town. Evidence of its former economic fortunes are all around, from workers' terraced houses to the old mills and the largely restored Rochdale Canal. Opened in 1804, this 33 mile long artery provided the first trans-Pennine link, enabling vessels to travel all the way from Hull to Liverpool. By 1830, the canal carried some 900,000 tons of freight.

This walk takes us along a short stretch of the revitalised canal, where you can inspect two of the ninety-two locks along the route, up to the edge of Inchfield Moor, giving long vistas of Todmorden to the north and the ancient deer park of Walsden Moor to the east. The downward route passes a working mill in Ramsden Clough and a facet of Yorkshire life that I have seen nowhere else in the county. How many tripe and elder works do you know?

The Waggon and Horses

This comfortable, family-run pub shares the valley bottom with a railway and the Rochdale Canal. Once the favourite roost of mill workers whose nearby terraced housing still makes cosy homes, it has a deserved local reputation for its 'sizzler' meals, the theme embracing chicken, beef steaks, pork and fish. Closed on Mondays, the pub is open on Tuesday to Friday from 12 noon to 3 pm and 5 pm to 11 pm; on Saturday from 11 am to 11 pm; and Sunday hours are 12 noon to 10.30 pm. Telephone: 01706 813318.

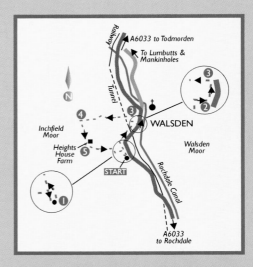

The Walk

① Turn left from the pub along the footway and walk on round the bend towards the prominent church spire. Cross the railway bridge and, opposite the premises of C&G Motors, cross the A6033 right, going forward by the gable of a terrace house to the Rochdale Canal towpath.

② Turn left by the lock (Nip Square Lock No 29) and continue along the towpath to the next lock (Travis Mill Lock No 28), passing the rear of the beer garden of the Cross Keys pub.

③ Turn left away from the canal and re-cross the A6033, continuing straight forward uphill on Inchfield Road. Ignoring a succession of footpaths to the left, keep climbing until you reach the Heights House Farm sign.

④ Go left along a track, following a public bridleway sign towards the farm. Bear left at the farm buildings.

⑤ Go through a gate and continue on a

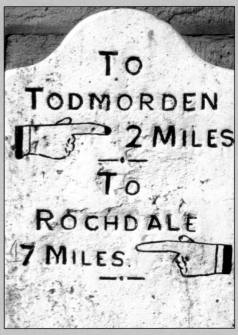

An old milestone, Walsden

The Rochdale Canal

descending packhorse route above the mill. Drop down and go through a gate, forking right and weaving down left and right, following a fence down to a gate. Go through left and emerge at Bailey's Tripe and Elder Works. Swing right over the beck and go left down Ramsden Wood Road to the A6033. Turn right, back to the pub.

PLACES OF INTEREST NEARBY

On the route of this walk is the **Heights House Farm Trail Riding Centre**. They can organise trail rides of two hours' duration and more onto Inchfield Moor and beyond. Telephone: 01706 818010. Also on the route is the extensive **Calderbank Nurseries and Garden Centre** in Walsden. Open every day.

Greetland

BIRD'S EYE VIEWS AND A FOLLY FLUE

The Sportsman's Inn

MAP REF: OS LANDRANGER 104 (GR 073213)	WALK 24	DISTANCE: 2 MILES

DIRECTIONS TO START: GREETLAND IS SOUTH OF HALIFAX. GO NORTH FROM JUNCTION 24 OF THE M62 TO ELLAND ON THE A629 AND TAKE THE B6114 AND THE B6113 WEST TO GREETLAND. THE PUB IS A THIRD OF A MILE WEST OF THE BUILT UP AREA. **PARKING:** PARK IN THE PUB CAR PARK.

South of the River Calder on a high bluff, Greetland has a bird's eye view of the valley and Halifax beyond. A Roman altar was discovered here in 1597 and there is still some conjecture as to whether the fabled Cambodunum was located here. Once a fashionable address for Halifax mill owners who built a number of typical stone mullioned and transomed properties in the vicinity, including Crawstone Hall, Greetland retains its distinguished and spacious air at the edge of an expansive moor.

This short and untaxing walk crosses the edge of Greetland Moor, visiting the local beauty spot of North Dean Wood. There are tremendous views all the way, the skyline of Halifax with its towers, steeples and chimneys being particularly fascinating. One building dominates the attention. Wainhouse's Folly Chimney is probably the weirdest structure in the entire county. Soaring to 275 ft it was built to vent smoke from the Washer Lane Dyeworks. It is smothered in Gothic ornamentation.

The Sportsman's Inn

In a commanding position at the edge of Greetland Moor, this stone-built inn has been altered many times over the years, blocked up windows and doorways attesting to a long history. Spacious inside with a large banqueting suite and open fires in the winter months, it has a comprehensive menu boasting everything from a 'bar snack to a banquet'. Roast beef and Yorkshire pudding is a firm favourite alongside such dishes as poached lemon sole, oriental stir fry, chicken in a red wine and bacon sauce and mixed vegetable chilli. The Sportsman's has a similar wide choice of ales – Mansfield, Timothy Taylor Landlord, Old Speckled Hen, Old Mill and Marston's Pedigree. Daily opening times are 12 noon to 11 pm (10.30 pm on Sundays). Telephone: 01422 373725.

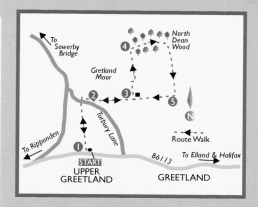

The Walk

① Turn right from the pub and go immediately right again, following a public bridleway sign. Continue to Turbury Lane and turn right along the lane, using the footway, for 200 yards.

② Turn left, following a public bridleway sign and continuing along a track at the edge of Greetland Moor.

③ Turn left at the side of the cottage,

The Victoria Mill (courtesy of Andy Thornton Architectural Antiques)

PLACES OF INTEREST NEARBY

Wainhouse's Folly Chimney in Wakefield Gate, King Cross, Halifax (access off Wakefield Road – A6026) is open to the public on selected Sundays and bank holidays. It was built at a cost of £15,000, its intricate detailing including a spiral staircase and a fabulous balcony. But have you enough puff? It has 400 steps! Telephone 01422 359454 for opening times.

To the east of the Sportsman's Inn in Victoria Mills, Stainland Road, Greetland are the **premises of Andy Thornton**, the converted mill holding the world's largest stock of architectural antiques and unusual décor. This amazing treasure house has everything – panelling, fire surrounds, doors, pews, pub and shop fittings, stained glass, furniture and lighting, garden ornaments and several kitchen sinks. Open every day. Telephone: 01422 377314.

Farming bric-a-brac at Victoria Mill (courtesy of Andy Thornton Architectural Antiques)

following a footpath sign to 'North Dean Wood'. The view to the north takes in the fantastic Wainhouse Chimney (see Places of Interest Nearby). Turn right wallside and go left in the field corner, following a wall down.

④ Cross a stile right and follow the ridge top in the woodland, dropping down left. Swing right and pass in front of the bungalow, merging with a broader track from the left by a yellow-arrow-marked post. Swing right on a track, following the Calderdale Way sign, keeping right towards the power lines to Moor Bottom Lane.

⑤ Turn right, following a public bridleway sign, and merge with the outward route, returning to the pub.

Wakefield

A MERRIE GO ROUND

Henry Boon's

MAP REF: OS LANDRANGER 104 (GR 328205)	WALK 25	DISTANCE: 1 1/2 MILES

DIRECTIONS TO START: WAKEFIELD IS SOUTH OF LEEDS AND HAS EXCELLENT ACCESS OFF THE M62, M1 AND A1. THE PUB IS IN PARLIAMENT STREET OFF WESTGATE, JUST BELOW THE RAILWAY STATION ON THE LEFT. **PARKING:** PARK IN THE LONG STAY 'PAY AND DISPLAY' CAR PARK IN DRURY LANE.

Known in ancient texts as the 'Merrie City' famed for its mystery plays, Wakefield has been a centre of commerce, industry and local government for centuries, its imposing 14th century cathedral of All Saints, together with a cluster of more recent civic buildings and an elegant Georgian square, giving this surprising city a wealth of interest. Built in a prominent hilltop position above the River Calder on whose medieval Wakefield Bridge will be found one of only four surviving chantry chapels in England, Wakefield has an impressive skyline dominated by the cathedral spire.

This short city ramble along some of Wakefield's more historic streets touches the lives of just a handful of the famous characters – an internationally acclaimed sculptress, a man who is credited with the introduction of modern anaesthetics and an author to rival Dickens.

Henry Boon's

In a licensed trade increasingly dominated by the conglomerates, Henry Boon's is a rare breed. A thoroughly independent alehouse, it is owned by the adjacent Clark's Brewery, serving home-brewed real ales and guest beers in traditional surroundings. What it lacks in more solid refreshments, Henry Boon's makes up for in its range of beers that includes Beer Festival medal winner Clark's Traditional Bitter, Festival Ale, Rams Revenge and T'Owd Dreadnought. Wakefield has a host of food outlets to complement the ale and a food court in the Ridings Centre, passed on this walk. Henry Boon's opening times are 11 am to 11 pm every day (10.30 pm on Sundays). Telephone: 01924 378126.

The Walk

① Go left from the pub along Parliament Street towards Wakefield Prison. In its grounds, once grew a solitary mulberry bush. Exercising prisoners, who circled its circumference every morning, gave rise to the popular nursery rhyme. Turn right on Back Lane and pass under the railway bridge. The property on the left is known as the Orangery. This was built in the early 1760s as a hothouse for fruit. Continue uphill, passing the Library. Almost anonymous at its rear is the entrance to the John Goodchild Collection, an archive of one million documents detailing the commercial and industrial life of the district.

② Go left on Cliff Parade and pass by the rear of County Hall on Burton Street,

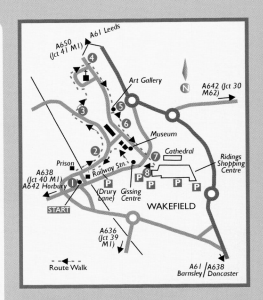

swinging left past the college on Cliff Hill.

③ Do not descend but turn right on Sandy Walk, going right at its end down a footpath. Turn left on Margaret Street to St John's Square. When it was erected in 1790, this speculative development on a remote plot some distance from the heart of the city was a risky financial gamble. Explore the square and St John's church.

④ Turn right along Wentworth Street, crossing the street and passing the hospital to reach the corner with Wentworth Terrace. On this corner, we will meet with the first of our celebrities, the work of sculptress Barbara Hepworth being displayed in the rear garden of the Art Gallery. The gallery houses an important collection of 19th and 20th century art (free entry). Open every day apart from Monday. Telephone: 01924 305900.

St John's church, Wakefield

⑦ Cross the traffic light controlled junction and fork left down Cross Street. On your right is an old pub – the Black Rock – that honours Wakefield district's coal mining heritage. Continue to the cathedral. At 247 ft its spire is the highest in Yorkshire. Fork right and visit the Ridings Centre – 90 retail outlets and a food court. Make your way back to the entrance.

⑤ Go left down Wentworth Terrace for a short distance and turn right down Laburnum Road, past the Police headquarters complex.

⑥ Turn right on Bond Terrace, crossing the road to Castrop-Rauxel Square. Displayed here is a much larger work by Barbara Hepworth. Go left into the Civic Quarter down Wood Street. The monumental County Hall in front was erected between 1894 and 1898 to accommodate the administrative machinery for the West Riding. Pass the equally impressive Court House and Town Hall, visiting the next building, the former Mechanics Institute – now Wakefield Museum (free entry). The museum rejoices in the work of the second of our heroes – Charles Waterton. An 18th century explorer, pioneering taxidermist and creator of the concept of nature reserves, this eccentric experimented with curare as an anaesthetic. The museum is open every day – afternoons only on Sundays. Telephone: 01924 305351. Continue along Wood Street to the junction.

⑧ Fork left down Kirkgate, walk on and merge with Marygate for 200 yards, crossing the road and turning right, following the sign to the 'Gissing Centre' down Thompson's Yard. On your right is the birthplace of the third of our celebrities – the Victorian novelist and roué George Gissing. The centre houses displays of his work and associated memorabilia. Open on Saturdays from April to October. Free admission. Telephone: 01924 255047. Weave left over the car park to Cheapside and walk on to Cliff Parade, turning left on the outward route back to the pub.

PLACES OF INTEREST NEARBY

On the outskirts of Wakefield (going south, take the A61, crossing the river and keeping left on the A638, then the next left on the A655 signposted to Normanton) is the conservation village of **Heath**. Its houses and cottages were built mainly in the 17th and 19th centuries. Heath has a very special period pub, the King's Arms. One of its atmospheric bars is lit by gaslight. Telephone: 01924 377527.

Midgley

A TRUNK ROUTE

The Black Bull

MAP REF: OS LANDRANGER 110 (GR 273146)	WALK 26	DISTANCE: 4½ MILES

DIRECTIONS TO START: THE BLACK BULL IS PROMINENTLY SITUATED AT THE JUNCTION OF THE A637 AND THE B6117 AT MIDGLEY, SOUTH-WEST OF WAKEFIELD, NEAR TO JUNCTIONS 38 AND 39 OF THE M1.
PARKING: PARK IN THE INN CAR PARK.

With long distance views over the Calder valley, the lofty hamlet of Midgley straddles a minor road overlooking the village of Netherton. On all points of the compass, it is encircled by extensive woods, fine forest walks through a number of local beauty spots and nature reserves making the area popular with walkers from nearby Wakefield and elsewhere. Following glade, forest edge and field paths, this relaxing saunter takes you to the lovely Coxley Valley, returning through Netherton and over a little used farm road.

The Black Bull

Out to pasture on the edge of Midgley, this strategically placed hostelry shares its name with a nearby farm. Much extended and improved in recent years, it displays original roof timbers and several old fireplaces, the rustic ambience emphasised by rescued farming implements and country prints. With five inter-connecting rooms, the large and accommodating inn is big on dining space, the varied menu including beef in red wine, lamb curry, pork in pepper, teriyaki steak, salmon fillet and a range of filled baguettes. The ale choices are Whitbread Trophy and Boddingtons. Daily opening times are 11 am to 11 pm (Sundays 12 noon to 10.30 pm). Telephone: 01924 830260.

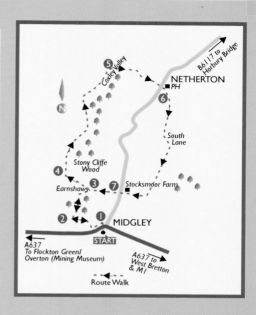

The Walk

① Cross the road from the pub (carefully – busy A road) and go left on the footway to cross the junction with Stocksmoor Road. Continue on the footway round the Bar Lane bend for 100 yards and go right, following a public footpath sign over a wall. Continue along a field edge and go left over a second stile and turn right, following the field edge to a gate. Go forward and drop down into a wood, cross a ditch on a bridge and swing left on a concrete path, following a public footpath sign. Walk on towards a gate and the wood edge.

② The next section of the route, shown on the sketch map, is not indicated on the OS map, a well-signposted diversion through the premises of Earnshaw's giving pedestrians an unexpected opportunity to enjoy their garden and timber products centre. Stay in the wood and turn right. Follow a yellow arrow marker through the nature reserve, weaving down and left to the garden centre, following the sign right. Leave the premises.

③ Just beyond the Earnshaw's entrance

PLACES OF INTEREST NEARBY

At Overton (go west from the pub and turn right in Flockton Green to the A642), the **National Coal Mining Museum for England** is an award-winning attraction that graphically illustrates our mining heritage in a series of exhibits and underground tours guided by a local miner. Warm shoes and sensible clothes are recommended. Other facilities include a shop, café bar and nature trail. Open every day apart from Christmas and the New Year. Telephone: 01924 848806.

The National Coal Mining Museum, Overton (courtesy of Wakefield MDC)

④ Turn right, following a marker, and walk on a woodland edge path for just over $^1/_2$ mile to the wood corner. Fork right off the main path away from the stile and keep along the woodland perimeter, crossing a stile and arcing left on the edge of a field, following the twisting course of the stream and crossing further stiles to a footbridge.

⑤ Turn right over the bridge into the wood. Swing right and keep right at the fork, climbing uphill to the steps. Climb and continue on a field edge path, crossing a further stile. Walk on into Netherton, crossing Coxley Crescent. Keep forward towards the Star public house.

sign, go left, following the signposted path into Stony Cliffe Wood, crossing a bridge. Follow the yellow arrow marker right to a kissing gate, going through left, crossing a footbridge and keeping forward uphill to a pair of old gate pillars at the woodland edge.

⑥ Cross the road and veer right down South Lane. Follow this quiet country lane for just over a mile, passing the cottages on the left and bearing right, passing Stocksmoor Farm, to the junction.

⑦ Walk forward across the B6117 and follow the Earnshaw's access drive, dropping down to the outward route and the pub.

Clayton West

A RIVER RUNS TO IT

The Junction

MAP REF: OS LANDRANGER 110 (GR 258115)	**WALK 27**	DISTANCE: $4\frac{3}{4}$ MILES

DIRECTIONS TO START: CLAYTON WEST IS ON THE A636 BETWEEN WAKEFIELD AND DENBY DALE, WEST OF THE M1 (JUNCTIONS 38/39). **PARKING:** PARK IN THE INN CAR PARK TO THE REAR (OR AT THE YORKSHIRE SCULPTURE PARK – SEE BELOW – STARTING THE WALK AT POINT 6).

Dog-eared maps reveal the industrial heritage of this surprisingly rural part of West Yorkshire, the word 'Mine' spreading over the contours like a rash. In 1855, the county had 333 collieries with a combined output of nearly 8 million tons. Over a century on, the new editions of the Ordnance Survey show flushes of green, coalfields giving way to newly restored meadows and woods. Clayton West had its own mine – Park Mill Colliery – on the fast sprouting hill behind the Junction pub.

This gentle field paths walk along parts of the Dearne Way, takes us to Bretton Hall and the acclaimed Yorkshire Sculpture Park set in a sylvan and romantic landscape of rolling hills, woodlands and lakes. Adequate time should be allowed for exploration of the park and perhaps refreshment in the Bothy Café.

The Junction

A local institution that was once in the shadow of Park Mill Colliery, this traditional pub has a small but inviting parlour with an open fire for the winter months. The coal dust has gone but the Junction still concentrates on the serious business of slaking thirsts, offering no food but two ales – Stones and Tetley. Daily opening times are 12 noon until 11 pm with the exception of Wednesdays – 6 pm to 11 pm. Telephone: 01484 865117.

Food can be had at the Bothy Café, halfway through this walk in the grounds of the Yorkshire Sculpture Park. Serving a selection of home-made hot meals, cakes and snacks, the café is open every day from 11 am. Telephone: 01924 830302.

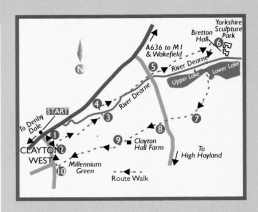

The Walk

① Cross the road from the pub and walk up the lane, continuing for 500 yards.

② Swing hard left down Back Lane. Pass the cricket pitch and keep going forward on a track, arcing right by the factory. Where the path forks, go left and follow the blue arrow marker 'Dearne Way'. Keep forward through a gate on a path between a fence and a hedge, cross a stile and follow the path right fieldside, crossing a second stile right and merging with a concrete path. Walk on to the treatment works.

③ Turn left on a lane and cross over the River Dearne on a bridge, proceeding for 250 yards after the bridge.

④ Turn right over a stile into a field, following an arrow marker, and continue down the middle of the field, veering slightly left for the top corner. Cross a stile right and swing right to the Dearne bank to a third stile. Cross and veer left away from the river to cut off the field corner to a fourth stile. Cross to a lane.

⑤ Follow the public footpath sign through a wall gap down two steps left. Weave left through a copse to a stile. Cross and keep left fenceside to the

PLACES OF INTEREST NEARBY

Entry to the **Yorkshire Sculpture Park** is free but there is a car parking charge. Set in 500 acres of 18th century landscaped grounds, this unique attraction presents a constantly changing international programme of sculptural exhibits – both traditional and modern – in an outstanding parkland setting. Open every day of the year. Telephone: 01924 830302.

The **Kirklees Light Railway** links Clayton West with Skelmanthorpe. This narrow gauge attraction has mini steam trains running every weekend and every day from Easter to mid September. Telephone: 01484 865727.

The tranquil setting of the Yorkshire Sculpture Park (courtesy of Wakefield MDC)

corner and the footpath sign, going left to a footbridge. Cross the Bentley Brook right and go left uphill to a stile on the skyline. Cross and keep forward, following the waymarker over a field. Continue forward alongside the hedge and at the field corner cross a stile to the track and the 'Clayton West' footpath sign.

⑥ Turn right on the track, walking on and going through an ornamental gate. Go forward. The signed entrance to the Yorkshire Sculpture Park is on the left. Cross the bridges over the Dearne and the lake's cascade and walk on right uphill to the next gate, going through and up on a farm track for 500 yards.

⑦ Turn right off the track, crossing a stile and following a white arrow marker. Head right over the large field for the trees in the corner to a stile and cross into a smaller field, following a hedge down to the side of a cottage. Cross via wall steps to a lane and go left for 150 yards.

⑧ Turn right, following a public footpath sign over the wall steps, and cross a field, walking on over a bridged ditch to the next field. Keep hedgeside, continuing to the right of Clayton Hall Farm, and swing right over the farmyard on a track to a junction of paths.

⑨ Keep forward, following the 'Kirklees Way' sign. At the field corner go right over a stile, following the 'Kirklees Way' sign left downhill, heading for the Emley Moor mast. After 150 yards, go left over a stile, dropping downhill to a planked bridge. Keep forward hedgeside and swing left in the corner, crossing a series of stiles and fields onto Millennium Green. Keep forward by the brick 'heritage wheel' and go through a kissing gate, keeping forward to Scott Hill.

⑩ Turn right and drop down the lane, back to the pub.

Denby Dale

PIES AND PACKHORSES

The White Hart

| MAP REF: OS LANDRANGER 110 (GR 228085) | WALK 28 | DISTANCE: 2½ MILES |

DIRECTIONS TO START: DENBY DALE IS 7 MILES WEST OF BARNSLEY ON THE A635.
PARKING: PARK IN THE PUB CAR PARK OR IN THE FREE CAR PARK NEARBY.

World famous for its gigantic pies celebrating everything from the recovery of King George III from madness in 1788 to the new millennium, Denby Dale grew up as a grey, linear weaving town alongside the River Dearne. For hundreds of years until the 17th century, the village cottages would purr to the rock and creak of spinning wheels and primitive hand-looms. Then came the discovery of steam power and vast reserves of local coal, industrialisation driving the building of great dams and mills all along the valley floor. With the explosion in economic activity came the railway, a magnificent viaduct still dominating the village.

From busy Denby Dale, this short walk climbs through ancient woodland to the hilltop settlement of Upper Denby, using an historic packhorse track. Much quieter than its neighbour, this pleasant village has a popular pub – the Dunkirk – the Rockwood Hunt meeting in its car park every Boxing Day. In the late 1660s two infamous witches were said to reside in the village, the names Susan Hinchliffe and Anne Shillitoe still frightening children to this day.

The White Hart

Perched over a busy crossroads in the heart of Denby Dale, the White Hart is a popular village local serving sandwiches and traditional bar food such as steak and kidney pie, scampi and burgers. The house ales are Tetley and a revolving guest beer. Opening times Monday to Wednesday are 12 noon to 3.30 pm and 7 pm to 11 pm. Thursday to Sunday hours are 12 noon to 11 pm (10.30 pm on Sundays). Telephone: 01484 862357.

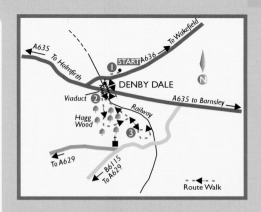

The Walk

①Turn right from the pub and go left, following the sign to Springfield Mill and Holy Trinity church. Go straight forward, following the public footpath sign. Pass the church and go through a wall gap. Keep forward over the rough amenity area and go through a wicket gate to the road. Turn right, using the footway, passing under the railway viaduct.

②Turn left, following a public bridleway sign. Turn right into Hagg Wood, going through a gate, and take the right fork, climbing uphill. Swing left and drop down to a wall then swing right on a setted path, climbing up, passing a bench.

③Merge left with a track in disrepair and turn left down Smithy Hill. Go left down Coal Pit Lane towards the playing field and then left by the barn (cockerel weather vane on top) along a path. Keep straight on between the houses and go through a wicket gate into a field. The prominent structure on the skyline to the north is the Emley Moor television transmission tower. Go

An old packhorse trail near Upper Denby

Emley Moor, near Denby Dale (courtesy of Wakefield MDC)

through a gate gap into a second field and go through a further wall gap. Turn right on the outward route. Instead of turning left off the setted track into the wood, keep on fenceside, dropping down to the road. Turn right on the outward route, back to the pub.

PLACES OF INTEREST NEARBY

This walk passes one of Denby Dale's old mills. **Springfield Mill** has now been converted for commercial use, offering an array of outlets including a children's play centre and a coffee shop. Open Monday to Saturday.

Holmfirth

'... WHERE THE FAMOUS TRIO LOAFED AND TINKERED'

The Postcard

MAP REF: OS LANDRANGER 110 (GR 143086)	WALK 29	DISTANCE: 3 MILES

DIRECTIONS TO START: HOLMFIRTH IS ON THE A635 AROUND 15 MILES WEST OF THE M1 (JUNCTIONS 37 AND 38). **PARKING:** PARK IN THE PAY AND DISPLAY CAR PARK ADJACENT TO THE PUB.

Through the power of television, Holmfirth is famous as the home of the hit series *Last of the Summer Wine*. Coveting the level ground in the valley of the River Holme, this modern tourist town under the shadow of high hills once earned its living from cloth making and farming. Alternative employment then came from an unlikely source, picture postcard production by the celebrated Balmforth Company heralding a change in fortune that today sees thronged Holmfirth bursting at the corset seams. Everyone, it appears, wants to be photographed on Nora Batty's steps!

I will take you there, but first we will see something of the surrounding countryside, tramping the hallowed tracks where the famous trio loafed and tinkered. We will pass by the river and a still working mill, returning to the town on the trail of those woollen stockings and the work of an artist whose watercolour landscapes have brought him international acclaim.

The Postcard

This accommodating and relaxing, centrally-placed pub changed its name in honour of a holiday institution that for years raised saucy titters nationwide. Decorated with more sober examples of the genre, the Postcard is popular with tourists, serving speciality 'sizzler steaks' (beef, gammon and pork), chilli con carne, giant Yorkshire puddings and battered haddock. The ale choices are Black Sheep, Stones, Worthington, Caffrey's and Boddingtons. Opening times Monday to Saturday are 11.30 am to 11 pm. Sunday hours are 12 noon to 10.30 pm. Telephone: 01484 683460.

The Walk

① Turn left from the pub along Huddersfield Road and go left again down Victoria Street, weaving left across the busy junction to the right of the church. In the little square to the right of the church is the instantly recognisable Sid's Café. Go forward up the steps and veer left, swinging right up the cobbles and the steps. Go left up Bunkers Hill and swing right, climbing steeply past the Old Vicarage. Fork left along Underbank Old Road and turn right downhill near the second Underbank Old Road nameplate, descending on a cobble walkway to the Dunford Road. Turn right along the road for a few yards.

② Turn diagonally left, following a public footpath sign downhill, and cross a parking area to the right of the buildings. Climb uphill and follow the track left, arcing right to a lane.

③ Cross the lane, going straight forward, and pass Oakmount bungalow on a rough track, going left. Continue forward on the track, walking on past the farm buildings. Keep on, passing a detached barn.

④ Leave the track, going right through a gate, heading diagonally left over a field towards the farmhouse. Cross a stile right and continue down wallside to a gate opening. Go through left by an oak tree to the wall corner. Swing right by the wall

PLACES OF INTEREST NEARBY

Housed in a recently restored cinema that originally belonged to the Bamforth family, **The Holmfirth Picturedrome** has a constantly changing programme of film events. In addition to producing postcards, the family also made pioneering silent films using local people as actors. Holmfirth could have stolen a march on Hollywood if this early initiative had been pursued with more vigour. On the first floor of the Picturedrome is the **Holmfirth Postcard Collection**, sentimental cards from the First World War and saucy seaside favourites featuring big bossomed ladies and their henpecked husbands taking centre stage. The collection is open daily from April to October; weekends only in winter. Telephone: 01484 689759.

Nora Batty's and Compo's houses at Holmfirth

and cross a stile, dropping down steps to a lane. Turn left for 20 yards.

⑤ Go right off the lane, following a public footpath sign diagonally left on a track, and go left through a gate, following a yellow arrow marker. Cross a series of fields, going through wall gaps, to a wood. Keep left, passing an overgrown quarry, and gradually descend. Drop down right and go through a wall gap left, leaving the wood. Walk upstream on the river bank to a footbridge and cross right.

⑥ Turn right, following the river bank, and continue to the mill dam, going right and left round the dam towards the chimney.

⑦ Just before the chimney, fork right and re-cross the river on a second footbridge. Fork left uphill into the wood, merging with a more substantial path. Keep left. Go through a gate gap and leave the wood, turning left on a path and crossing back over the river to the road.

⑧ Turn right opposite the Victoria pub on Woodhead Road and walk on the footway back into Holmfirth, passing the studio of water colourist Ashley Jackson. Continue back to the pub.

Holme

RESERVOIR JOGS

The Fleece

MAP REF: OS LANDRANGER 110 (GR 108058)	WALK 30	DISTANCE: 2³/₄ MILES

DIRECTIONS TO START: HOLME IS 2¹/₂ MILES SOUTH-WEST OF HOLMFIRTH
ON THE A6024. **PARKING:** PARK IN THE PUB CAR PARK TO THE REAR.

At the frontier of a vast expanse of moors, this tiny settlement's lofty claim to fame is the nearby television station – the Holme Moss mast marking Yorkshire's eastern edge. At an elevation of 1,000 ft, Holme looks down the valley to neighbouring Holmbridge and Holmfirth. This lonely spot once rattled to the sound of hand-looms before the advent of industrialisation. Now only the wind rustles the serenity of this wildly beautiful place. With more than ample rain, the wilderness surrounding Holme is a veritable sponge, six reservoirs, including the infamous Bilberry, whose breaching in 1852 resulted in 81 deaths, providing an ocean of drinking water and some fine waterside paths.

This walk takes us across the delightful Netherley Clough for a circuit of Ramsden Reservoir, returning through a lovely second dell in Rake Dike.

The Fleece

This compelling pub should take a lead from many a petrol station. It should put out a sign reading: 'LAST CHANCE TO EAT FOR 15 MILES'. A former livery stable and a pub for over 200 years, the stone-built Fleece has inviting dining and bar areas serving a wide range of meals including steak and kidney pie, mushroom Stilton bake, fruity chicken curry, poached salmon, spaghetti carbonara and a range of steaks. The bar top line up is Burtonwood and Strongarm. The pub is closed on Mondays. Opening times Tuesday to Friday are 12 noon to 3 pm and 6 pm to 11 pm. Weekend openings are 12 noon to 11 pm (10.30 pm on Sundays). Telephone: 01484 683449.

The Walk

① Turn right from the pub for 20 yards and go left, following a public footpath sign. Swing right and go through a wall gap at the side of a garden, proceeding through a gate into a meadow. Go through a wall gap and drop down to the Gill Hey Bridge over the Rake Dike.

② Cross on a footbridge and swing right up steps through bilberry, crossing a stile and heading up towards the trees. Follow a broken wall round and go through a wall gap, following a yellow arrow marker forward. Follow a broken wall down and go through a gate gap into the next field (the path is better on the right side of the wall). Keep following the broken wall and drop down a steep bank, going left over a stile to a footbridge over Netherley Clough.

③ Go left over the footbridge and left on a footpath, climbing towards the trees. Swing right

The leafy dell at Rake Dike

Digley reservoir, near Holme (courtesy of Wakefield MDC)

through a gate opening and cross a stile.

④ Go left on a track, passing between Riding Wood Reservoir and Ramsden Reservoir on the dam top.

⑤ Turn left, following a public footpath sign, and walk on the track past the

PLACES OF INTEREST NEARBY

Nearby **Holmfirth** has a number of attractions devoted to the hit TV series *Last of the Summer Wine*. An exhibition about the series, **Compo's World** – housed in what was Compo's house on Scarfold, off Hollowgate – is filled with photographs, memorabilia and some of the remarkable inventions dreamed up by the dynamic trio. Open every day. Telephone: 01484 681408.

amenity area on your right to the dam top between Ramsden Reservoir and Brownhill Reservoir.

⑥ Turn sharp left and turn right across the dam top. Swing right uphill and follow the path left, dropping down to the waterfall on Rake Dike.

⑦ Swing right over the footbridge uphill, continuing up to the marker post. Go left, following a yellow arrow marker to a stile. Cross and walk on to the next stile, crossing between a wall and a fence. Go left over a wall using the throughs, cross a further stile and follow a yellow arrow marker along a lane. Notice the remarkable troglodyte house on the left. Go left on the road, back to the pub.